The Concept of
ANXIETY

The Concept of

ANXIETY

*A Simple Psychologically Oriented
Deliberation in View of
the Dogmatic Problem of
Hereditary Sin*

SØREN KIERKEGAARD

Edited and Translated
with Introduction and Notes by
ALASTAIR HANNAY

Liveright Publishing Corporation
a Division of W. W. Norton & Company
New York • London

For information about permission to reproduce selections from this book,
write to Permissions, Liveright Publishing Corporation, a division of
W. W. Norton & Company, Inc., 500 Fifth Avenue, New York, NY 10110

For information about special discounts for bulk purchases, please contact
W. W. Norton Special Sales at
specialsales@wwnorton.com or 800-233-4830

Manufacturing by LSC Harrisonburg
Book design by JAM Design
Production manager: Devon Zahn

Library of Congress Cataloging-in-Publication Data

Kierkegaard, Søren, 1813–1855.
[Begrebet angest. English]
The concept of anxiety : a simple psychologically oriented deliberation in view of the
dogmatic problem of hereditary sin / Søren Kierkegaard ; edited and translated with
introduction and notes by Alastair Hannay. — First Edition.
pages cm
Includes bibliographical references.
ISBN 978-0-87140-719-1 (hardcover)
1. Sin, Original. 2. Psychology, Religious. 3. Anxiety—Religious aspects—Christianity. I. Hannay, Alastair, editor of compilation. II. Title.
BT720.K5213 2014
233'.14—dc23
2013037399

ISBN 978-1-63149-004-0 pbk.

Liveright Publishing Corporation, 500 Fifth Avenue, New York, NY 10110
www.wwnorton.com

W. W. Norton & Company Ltd., 15 Carlisle Street, London W1D 3BS

7 8 9 0

I would like to dedicate this
translation to my sister
Jane Wiebel

Contents

Translator's Introduction

Anxiety is life's inescapable accompaniment, its constant undertow. Every step we take offers it an opportunity; to avoid anxiety we would have to lock ourselves away. But who would then dare say we were not still anxious? The nineteenth-century Russian writer Nikolai Gogol's *Diary of a Madman* humorously describes the increasing insanity of a minor civil servant who, taken in care, begins to interpret everything around him as designed to comply with his wishes. Doors closed to him are for his protection, if they are open it is to facilitate his royal progress, and harsh treatment in the asylum is part of the ritual of coronation to the Spanish throne. If we may allow that madness can purge all anxiety, on this side of insanity there are those of us whose daily routines can be so ordered as also to arouse the suspicion that our lives are ruled not so much by the order we impose as by a persistent undercurrent of anxiety that explains the resort to rules. We are still anxious, anxious about anxiety. Even open defiance of anxiety, facing it head-on as in extreme sports, may be seen as a way of acknowledging its motivational power. But then it might also reveal something deeper, a need to focus on a particular danger to be overcome in order to clear the mind of possibilities we prefer not to fathom.

To many of us that might seem a good thing, even if the means appear drastic; although there appears to be nothing obviously pathological in defying danger, it is in a way therapeutic. A rush of adrenalin can give a welcome sense of well-being. But there are cases of unsuppressed anxiety that clearly spell some sort of disorder. They have been given labels: anxiety disorder—plain and simple—or more ominously, obsessive compulsive disorder and traumatic stress and social anxiety disorders. These merge with or are components in familiar phobias, such as agoraphobia, claustrophobia, and acrophobia, panicky desires to avoid large open spaces, small enclosures, and unusual heights. The treatments that psychologists and psychiatrists provide give sufferers a more circumscribed sense of their own existence, a greater sense of security in the here and now, and an indifference to what may come. Unlike that of those who face anxiety head-on by defying it, it is the indifference of someone for whom the possibilities that seem so alarming have been safely put out of mind.

Kierkegaard tells us that this is wrong. It is to turn our backs on possibilities upon which our human destinies may depend, spiritual possibilities that we are by nature prone to avoid and therefore naturally shun, but which we nevertheless have it in us to face. *The Concept of Anxiety* speaks of a dawning spirit or, in more concretely psychological terms, of a growing awareness of our peculiar status among living creatures as conscious of our own singularity, of not being in immediate continuity with our surroundings but in some way above or apart from them, able to see ourselves as selves in relation to the world, and to other selves with whom we share it. Perhaps, among the disorders mentioned here, those that come closest to anxiety in Kierkegaard's sense are the phobias, in particular a sense of catastrophic severance from one's relation to solid earth. In another way, Kierkegaard's anxiety is both like and unlike what is known as "generalized anxiety disorder," a form of disability in which there is no specific mental allergen as in the case of those phobias, but an indiscriminate anxiety in which anything that comes along causes worry. However, unlike GAD, which focuses on each particular as it comes, indeed on any particular, the anxiety in Kierkegaard's analysis "differs altogether from fear and similar concepts that refer to something definite."

In a suggestive rather than clear indication of what this anxiety is, we are told that it is "freedom's actuality as the possibility of possibility." In following the clue that the mention of freedom provides, we can begin to see what kind of generalized anxiety Kierkegaard is talking about, and also why he will claim that it is a misunderstanding to think of it as a "disorder" that can be treated with "pills and powders." It will turn out to be a global rather than a generalized anxiety that, rather than having anything or everything as its focus, is anxiety in the face of nothing. The metaphors drawn on to describe it can remind us of those phobias and of acrophobia in particular: "anxiety is the dizziness of freedom that emerges when spirit wants to posit the synthesis, and freedom now looks down into its own possibility and then grabs hold of finiteness to support itself."

Anxiety in this generalized form is not something to be cured by therapy; in fact "cure" is not the right word for its removal at all. Anxiety can be replaced only by the freedom whose harsh requirements are its cause. Being free requires us to release the brakes that anxiety represents in order to accept and appropriate our proper spiritual fulfillment or perhaps even to recognize, if that is what we in the end believe, that no such prospect is in store. Roughly, in *The Concept of Anxiety*, the dizzying height from which anxious spirit shrinks in its acrophobic panic should be grasped as the vantage-point from which the human being may achieve its proper fulfillment but in a nonfinite form. To use medication or such relaxation techniques as meditation and yoga, or just plain exercise, to reduce the effect of socially disabling and personally destabilizing forms of generalized anxiety is one thing; it is another to interrupt progress toward spiritual fulfillment by reducing levels of consciousness. To do so merely adds to the aggregate of what Kierkegaard here calls sinfulness, and to the "objective" anxiety that is consonant with it, that already exists in a society, and in the context of which every individual later than Adam loses innocence.

But why this reference to sin and to Adam? What is "hereditary sin" doing in the title and isn't it usually called "original"? How can the barbaric idea that this biblical figure is to blame for a point of departure for which we later humans have no responsibility be of any interest to our enlightened age, even to that element of it still tuned into religion?

The opening chapter of The *Concept of Anxiety* (henceforth *Anxiety*) puts some effort into sweeping aside that simple reading of the Genesis story. The point in doing so is to tell us that we are all in Adam's position, except that unlike Adam we do not begin from scratch in a state of unalloyed innocence. For we who come later, a sense of sinfulness is already fixed in ways, in habits and practices, that are charged with the sins of our predecessors, sins of authority as much as of disobedience, some of them also taken on by what passes for Christianity itself. But then Christianity, as Kierkegaard sees it, is not a topic for treatises. Nor do doctrine and ritual get to the content let alone core of true religion; ceremony and the intoning of words no more make a genuinely religious community than mere flag-waving makes a nation. Christianity, one of Kierkegaard's pseudonyms says elsewhere, is better understood as a form of communication, a way of associating based not on outward proof of membership but on an understanding of what it is to be a human being, with its deficits, trials, and hopes for fulfillment, and also fear of what is required to make good the human deficit. That complex fear, a fear that is also a longing, is the theme of this "simple" psychological deliberation.

But then there is sin. That bad conduct is to be understood as a violation of God's law sounds rebarbative in an age versed in Nietzsche and Freud, even to those of the Christian faith. Faithful Nietzscheans dispense with God in any case, the deity being a long-standing impediment to a new morality that exploits the possibilities of selfhood rather than, as Nietzsche reads traditional Christian morality, repressing them. As for Freudians, they will be seeking fulfillment in their personal happiness by removing more complicated hindrances to that end, since for them evil has something to do with unnecessary inhibitions in the way of healthy psychosomatic development. *Anxiety's* topic is also the malfunctioning psyche, but it says that proper psychic functioning depends on a balance between psyche and soma "sustained by spirit."

Kierkegaard's criticism of his society and its ways, inside and outside religion, does however bear comparison with Nietzsche's, and vice versa. The difference is that Nietzsche saw himself as clearing a space that leaves no room for God's comeback, while Kierkegaard's clearance is designed to allow God at last to have a look in. Both thinkers are products of the German Idealist tradition but in their different ways mark its ending. To grasp the reason for Kierkegaard's focus on hereditary sin, and its connection with anxiety, it helps therefore to look at the terms of that tradition, since it is these that he uses to oppose it. This fact can easily mislead one into supposing that *Anxiety* is a conscious parody dressed up as a treatise on anxiety simply to ridicule the very idea of attempting such a thing. From there it would be but a short step to suppose that nothing in it should be taken seriously. The reader may conclude that, on the contrary, never was there a more serious "treatise" on anxiety. It places anxiety where it belongs, in that dawning consciousness, peculiar to humankind, of a forced capacity to reflect on the manner of its own existence, among other things but somehow very centrally, on the nature or role of this very capacity. The complex purpose of this "deliberation" is to persuade us that the topic in question is too important to spend time finding a place for it in a system of thought. Kierkegaard's "essays [attempts]," "deliberations," "compilations," and "expositions" have an openly "unscholarly," that is to say in the term of the time "unscientific" style, signaling that rather than presenting views for further and in principle endless discussion, their purpose is to put readers back on track, to restore these topics to an "actuality" where the problem is faced head-on. Kierkegaard's plan of campaign can be said, in general, to be directed at retrieving such "topics" from the vicarious lives they have for centuries led in an intellectual arena as puzzles for clever minds, minds self-authorized to arrive at and dictate doctrines and patterns of behavior for the respectful or fearful to follow. Their proper place is as challenges in each individual's confrontation with the conditions of actual existence.

Anxiety (Danish *Angest*) was no new concept in the intellectual circles at the time Kierkegaard wrote. In his reading of the Romantics he would have come across the German "Angst" often enough. Philosophers, too, in the Romantic era helped themselves liberally to notions associated with mental conflict and stress in their dynamic visions of the way in which the world came about and is *en route*—even endlessly—to its fulfillment. At their center was the now seldom discussed Schelling (1775–1854), whose *System des transzendentalen Idealismus*[1] and subsequent works introduced the Absolute Idealism that engaged the attention of much of intellectual Europe in the early nineteenth century. In doing so it nurtured more familiar names: Hegel and Marx, but also Kierkegaard.

For Schelling, history was a series of stages emerging from a Fall which, much like a metaphysical edition of the big bang, accounts for the presence of sheer diversity out of nothing. Diversity seeks unity in its difference and unification is the goal of the continuing development. Humankind is a part of the diversity but also party to the unifying, at least in principle. Participation requires will or understanding or both. For this humankind finds a model in the ideal of a personal God, a God that is no human invention but rather, if an invention at all, one that the ground of all things has come up with itself. Briefly, the ground of all things forces itself into the shape of personality so that humankind, through imitation, may contribute to the continuing creation which then becomes also its own fulfillment. A long footnote in Chapter 2 of *Anxiety* tells us that in Schelling's works "there is often talk of anxiety, wrath, anguish, suffering etc.," something that Kierkegaard refers to a little cheekily as "the deity's creative birth pangs." But he warns us not to confuse these agonizings with those that follow the "positing of sin."

Hegel (1770–1831), once a student-friend of Schelling's, his younger colleague to whom much of his earlier thinking was indebted, retained this "conflict" terminology in his own rationalistic version of spiritual emergence. This was one in which the personal God dissolves pantheistically, or some would say altogether, into the developing world as we find it, this now being where, if at all, we find the divine will at work. In the *Phenomenology* we read, in connection with the development of self-conscious spirit as separate from the world it surveys:

> With the positing of a single particular . . . [consciousness establishes] the beyond . . . [and in this way] suffers violence at its own hands, [spoiling] its own limited satisfaction. When consciousness feels this violence, its anxiety [*Angst*] may well make it retreat from the truth, and strive to hold on to what it is in danger of losing. . . . If it wishes to remain in a state of unthinking inertia, then thought troubles its thoughtlessness, and its own unrest disturbs its inertia. Or, if it entrenches itself in sentimentality . . . [etc.][2]

Anxiety's reader will find these words, and at least one metaphor, almost exactly reproduced in the second chapter in an account of "Subjective Anxiety." But where the gist of Hegel's philosophy was, through rational conceptualization of the human situation and its continuing history, to restore the belief that thought captures reality as it is, Kierkegaard polemicizes fiercely in the other direction. As the epigraph to *Anxiety* puts it, the age of distinctions is over; all distinction can be reconciled, even that between subject and object. *Anxiety* fights that view. Self-conscious spirit apprehends a beyond that it knows thought cannot possibly reach, but for which it nonetheless has a longing, although in a more personal and full-blooded way than that provided in thought. But this it can do only at the cost of all familiar means of self-identity. Anxiety is the ambiguous mood in which spirit becomes self-conscious in this gap-widening setting. Hegel talks negatively of the "sighs and prayers" of religion. To him they merely indicate that consciousness has so far failed to see the "true identity of inner and outer."[3] For Kierkegaard (in this respect as well as others coming closer to Kant, of whose thought he speaks with respect) that failure is inevitable and should not only be accepted but exploited to spiritual advantage. One way of reading not just *Anxiety* but the preceding and succeeding pseudonymous works is as a many-sided attempt to replace the still dominant Romantic view of religion with another that acknowledges the great strain that religious belief puts upon the understanding.

A further footnote, this one on *Anxiety*'s final page, refers to a writer, Johann Georg Hamann (1730–88), a main proponent of the late eighteenth-century *Sturm und Drang* (sometimes translated "Storm and Stress") movement. Hamann had been Kierkegaard's own early inspiration in the matter of subjectivity. The footnote recalls Hamann's characterization of *Angst* as an "impertinent disquiet and holy hypochondria," something described with Hamann's characteristic pungency as the "fire with which we season sacrificial animals in order to preserve us from the putrefaction of the current *seculum* [century]." In a journal entry from two years prior to *Anxiety*'s publication and only a few months after returning from a prolonged stay in Berlin, where among other things he had attended Schelling's famous lectures and also written a considerable portion of the second part of *Either/Or*, Kierkegaard writes that he regrets both that Hamann had not pursued this thought and that he had not understood it in the way that he, Kierkegaard, would prefer.[4] In that same entry we can get a sense of Kierkegaard's preferred understanding. It contains his first recorded pondering on the role of anxiety in relation to sin:

> Now people have often enough treated the nature of original sin, and yet they have lacked a principal category, namely *anxiety*; this is its essential determinant. Anxiety is in fact a desire for what one fears, a sympathetic antipathy; anxiety is an alien power that seizes the individual, and yet one cannot tear oneself free of it and one does not want to, for one fears, but what one fears is what one desires. Anxiety now renders the individual powerless, and the first sin always takes place in powerlessness; therefore it apparently lacks accountability, but this lack is the actual snare.

So *Anxiety*'s topic can be traced in its time from a Romantic concern with the power of passions to reveal the nature of reality in both literature and philosophy and through a vision of the world in which a personal God shows the way to human participation in the further completion of the creation. But according to Kierkegaard (or his pseudonym Johannes Climacus in *Concluding Unscientific Postscript*) we cannot find God in the creation, and for that reason knowledge of good and evil is not to be found there either. That is the meaning of the Fall.

Kierkegaard's psychology is unlike any scientific discipline that goes by that name today. It is essentially Hegelian in its structure and aims, though again anti-Hegelian in its stress on the individual subject. Psychology was for Hegel a science of "subjective spirit," its topic that same dynamic of spiritual emergence we find in Schelling. But in Hegel's case the dynamics (or the "dialectic") are described exclusively in terms of humankind's developing self-awareness. The point of view is that of a historical consciousness. Spiritual advance at any historical moment is manifested in existing institutions. These, along with the existing social morality, express the result, so far, of a progressively rational historical development under the name of "objective spirit." According to Hegel, it is through participation in and adherence to current institutions and morality that individual subjects become themselves. A science of *subjective* spirit has little to do positively except take note that individuals as a rule instantiate a degree of objective spiritual development, which is perhaps why *Anxiety* can say, "We hardly ever see the concept of anxiety treated in psychology." Any exceptions are to be explained in terms of what they lack and psychology has of course a pathology up its sleeve, taking note of the fact that individuals may not conform to objective spirit. Positively, for Hegel, subjective spirit is the locus of the individual conscience, through which the objective spiritual environment realizes its directives, or as that in which objective spirit is expressed at the level of consciousness. The source of evil is the individual conscience's failure to be such an expression and to take the question of good and evil into its own hands. Since, or if, the existing order is a manifestation of God's will, taking things into one's own hands is to perpetrate what the author of *Fear and*

Trembling, referring directly to Hegel's account in *Philosophy of Right*, calls a "moral form of evil."[5]

A science of subjective spirit for Kierkegaard is quite the opposite. The choice between good and evil rests with subjective spirit. Kierkegaard therefore had to resist giving the impression that his emphasis on the passion of faith in the face of the absurd meant that he was just a Romantic who had brought Christianity and a personal relation to God into the picture merely to add a touch of personal responsibility. Good and evil are still "knowledge," but it is available only to what *Anxiety*'s companion work *Philosophical Crumbs* (or *Fragments*) calls "a new organ," namely faith.[6] For Kierkegaard a science of subjective spirit is vital in the interests of greater self-awareness: "Psychology is what we need and above all a sound knowledge of human life and sympathy for its interests." Acquiring that knowledge is a "task to be solved before there can be any question of completing a Christian view of life."[7] But the Christian view of life is not included in the science. As *Anxiety*'s Introduction makes clear, the science stands on its own feet before handing over its results to "dogmatics."

The psychologist here is an observer of ordinary life and can look into or even write literature based on observation and hypotheses based on personal experience but also testable in their projected implications: "Someone who has occupied himself with psychology, and with psychological observation, according to some standard will have acquired a general human flexibility that enables him at once to construct his example which, even if lacking factual authority, has an authority of another kind." It is not to the rare case that the psychologist looks but to things that "happen everywhere . . . and every day if only the observer is present."

And yet, in this work, the psychologist's topic is indeed discussed from the point of view of someone in whose growing self-awareness there comes a point when sin is "posited." *Anxiety*'s observations are from that point of view. The trajectory of its deliberation is indicated in a further quotation from the journal entry calling for a "sound knowledge of human life and sympathy for its interests":

> In what sense is the sensuous, or rather sexuality, sin? If every Sunday one preaches a love which is spirit and truth, letting the erotic disappear as though it were nothing, then marital relations will become so spiritual that the sexual is forgotten and the cloister or abstinence will be far truer. What is to be made of it all if with the Church's consent we visit the theater in the evening and hear the erotic extolled? We are not supposed to go into the monastery but to marry. Right, but that is a rather foolish thing to do if the highest expression of marital love is a love unconcerned with sex.

Whether science or not, even Kierkegaardian psychology does not reach to the human core, which is the self that "no science knows" and is known only to itself.

But what interest is there today in psychological discussion, scientific in any sense or none, that has original or hereditary sin as its reference? Indeed what purpose other than cultural curiosity, or whatever other focus of what Kierkegaard disparagingly calls "interest," is served by retranslating a work published 170 years ago?

The answer must be given in the reading, but several things speak for the continued relevance of Kierkegaard's thoughts on the matter. He himself prophesied that what he called "the category of the single individual" would be his lasting contribution to history. He may be right. He called it his own category, as indeed it was, not only because he formed it in the way he did, but more importantly because it was born of his own experience. For him it was a religious category, something that in our own age strikes many readers as confining. Today we associate singularity with social and psychological isolation rather than with the requirements of a relationship to God. Or, in a more philosophical vein, we at most associate it with that offshoot of German Idealism that became known as Existentialism, and of which Kierkegaard is sometimes proclaimed to be the father.

In pointing to religion, *Anxiety* makes clear that its own concern is with the complex dynamics in which the human being awakens to its spiritual situation and to the needs to which religion responds. Although the New Testament is liberally cited and Christianity occasionally alluded to, *Anxiety*'s biblical focus is on the Old Testament story of Adam and Eve. The Genesis story in *Anxiety* is refashioned to epitomize what happens in every case of the dawning of spirit, except that in the course of time there is an accumulation of anxiety corresponding to the sinfulness that one generation inherits from its predecessor. Adam had no part in "objective" anxiety, but neither do we share with Adam any of his pristine innocence. We awaken spiritually to a world that through the centuries has accommodated itself to the trials of spirit. It has done so by making spirituality itself sound more easy and even fun, or, alternatively, by giving people ample opportunity to keep their minds off the larger existential worry. Not only amusements but whole ways of life have been cultivated that alleviate the restlessness or unease that any intimation of a spiritual destiny might cause. But these too place a host of other worries in their path. It can of course be, and has been, the case that such worries are avoided only by the rich or by those paid to talk incessantly of spiritual fulfillment. But the modern world is one in which events have overtaken the situation where work was a way of closing the mind. Widespread unemployment on the one hand and lives with extensive built-in leisure periods provide increasing exposure to the *ennui* that was once the doubtful privilege of the few. Boredom, says *Anxiety*, is "a continuity in nothingness." This point is brought home in the most elaborate discussion of anxiety, "Anxiety about the Good" or "the demonic," in Chapter IV.

The anxieties nowadays labeled "disorders" can themselves be nervous responses to ways of life unconsciously but strategically placed in the path of a greater fulfillment that is too hard to accept. Rather than accept it, we prefer to think of fulfillment in terms of restoring to our lives better ways of functioning in an increasingly complex world. We put off all thought of what it means to be a merely finite creature—until such times as we have to cope with that too, but then in ritual ways that allow us to extinguish that anguish as an unavoidable interlude.[8]

Martin Heidegger (1889–1976), the German existentialist philosopher and social critic, picks up *Anxiety*'s threads at this point. His project is descriptive, or "phenomenological," which means removing *Anxiety*'s psychology from the context of religion and translating it into a general account of the human being's inescapably finite situation. In an account a good deal less "simple" than Kierkegaard's seminal "deliberation," Heidegger offers a kind of critical prolegomena to any future theology. Anxiety, following Kierkegaard, is the mood in which human beings awaken to the peculiarly exposed vantage point they "enjoy" by virtue of their spe-

cifically reflective form of awareness, loosening an initially immediate tie with the world. Although Heidegger offers no reason of
the kind we find in Kierkegaard, in terms of a lost opportunity of
fulfillment, for why we should not avoid anxiety but face it, the
possibility of a theological view remains but with the finite limits of our lives in full view. Thus Heidegger can talk in *Sein und
Zeit* (1927) of an inauthentic immersion in everyday life (*Das Man*).
Authentic selfhood consists in "being toward death," where *Dasein*
(the German equivalent of *Tilværelse*, or human existence) acquires
an understanding of what it is to be a single human being and also
of a disposition to escape this insight by falling back into *Das Man*.
This abstract substantive is doubtless derived from Kierkegaard's
liberal use of "man," properly translated as "one" as in "one thought
that . . .", but convertible as often in the present translation into
the passive form "it was thought that . . ." Heidegger's expression
is sometimes translated as "the they." Relapsing from isolation into
Das Man is a source of guilt which through retrospection to the ini-
tial state of immersion is then directed also at that state. Readers
of *Anxiety* will note a considerable parallel here with Kierkegaard's
text and its treatment of guilt (prior to sin). It is indeed hard to
imagine what would remain of Heidegger's analysis of *Dasein* had
he not come across *Anxiety* and also Kierkegaard's own concentrated piece of social criticism in *A Literary Review*. From Heidegger's mining of these sources we can further trace the influence of
Kierkegaard on that arch-existentialist Jean-Paul Sartre (1905–80)
and his concept of the "singular universal." Both philosophers draw
what can be called anthropological conclusions from the inherent
presence in the human of a global anxiety, one that differs from a
generalized anxiety that focuses on specific events and situations
even though indiscriminatingly.

Sociologists too have concerned themselves with human singularity, but in terms of social and associated cultural causes. The dissolution of conditions of social belonging were stated in the late nineteenth century by the French sociologist Émile Durkheim with his notion of *anomie* (*Le Suicide*, 1897), sometimes called "normlessness." Just as Kierkegaard finds psychology a necessary preliminary to an understanding of the individual's relation to the promise of salvation, so Durkheim argues for the independent status of sociology as a science that can uncover facts irreducible to those of psychology. Kierkegaard might have agreed, so long as those facts of psychology were irreducible in turn. Max Weber, the German sociologist in whose circle Kierkegaard was seriously discussed, is well known for noting what he termed the "demystification of the world" (*Die protestantische Ethik und der Geist des Kapitalismus*, 1922). An atomizing of society leaves individuals with little but the power of reason, with which they dissolve the myths that once gave people and nations their psychological guarantees, but also reorganize society in productive ways designed to guarantee survival. Beyond the contentment that a well-organized society requires and therefore makes possible, at least for some people, no further questions arise of a deeper fulfillment.

Instead, fulfillment in the form of social guarantees of selfhood is found in some necessary "other," that is to say in some external authority to which the subject *is* subject, and what is a subject after all if not subjected to something? Increasingly in Kierkegaard the claim is that the other that establishes the self, to which the self is subject and acquires selfhood, is God. Fulfillment takes the form of faith, not as an act of allegiance or some special stance that would be merely a kind of flag-waving, but in actively following the will of God as revealed in the example of

Christ. Seeing how things were going in the direction later ana-
lyzed by the sociologists, Kierkegaard wrote in 1847 that "[t]he
evolution of the whole world tends in the direction of the absolute significance of the category of the particular." But that, for
Kierkegaard, "is precisely the principle of Christianity."[9] Others
might put this in another way, saying that the way the world is
going is one in which if Christianity had not been invented earlier, it would have been better to invent it now. But, regarding
invention, a passage in the concluding pages of *Anxiety*'s accompanying publication *Philosophical Crumbs* reads:

> No philosophy (because it concerns only the intellect), no
> mythology (because it concerns only the imagination), no
> historical knowledge (which concerns only memory) has
> ever got such an idea, which suggests that in this connec-
> tion one can make the ambiguous claim that it did not
> arise in any human heart.[10]

Christians must of course believe this. The Other that provides
the subject with its given ideal of selfhood cannot do its work if
it is thought to be merely a human device designed to do that.
No belief in God can be a belief in the believer's own invention.
Readers of Kierkegaard may not like his version of what they must
not believe they have invented, but any revision has to be believed
to be real.

   Kierkegaard knew firsthand the personal problems that occupy
psychiatry and since his time have interested philosophers and
sociologists. He interests us as much in his own acute powers of
psychological perception and self-observation as in the framework
within which he exercised them. One "thesis" that emerges from

this "simple" psychological deliberation is that psychological observation begins in the observer's self-awareness and broad experience of the ways of the psyche. There is a message here for much that goes for psychiatry in our day. What one may say of the author of *The Concept of Anxiety*'s place in our thought today is that, even if he predates official proclamations and analyses of the subject's separation from the guarantors of selfhood, his own activity with its personal background anticipates that very situation.

Translator's Note

The Concept of Anxiety (original title *Begrebet Angest*) was first published in June 1844. Kierkegaard had just turned thirty-one. The modest edition of 250 copies, half the number of the other pseudonymous works, was finally sold out eleven years later, whereupon a second edition of 500 copies was ordered and published in August 1855, just three months before Kierkegaard died at the age of forty-two. The second edition, on which the present translation is based, was unchanged except for some orthographic details and one serious blemish (corrected here) due to a typesetter mistaking a near pun for a double occurrence of the same word. It appears that Kierkegaard himself, who was otherwise occupied at the time and would soon fall fatally ill, made no changes to the text.[1]

Five days earlier that same June in 1844, and only nine months after *Fear and Trembling* and *Repetition*, along with several "Edifying Discourses," there also appeared a companion work already mentioned, *Philosophical Crumbs* (or *Fragments*). The two were composed in tandem, the latter with more attention to style and presumably written in less haste than *Anxiety*, which has been one of the least successfully translated of Kierkegaard's works. Its tightly expressed thought, some stylistic casualness, and occasional syntactical idiosyncrasies make it no easy task for the English-language translator, who already has to deal with the incongruities in sentence construction between Danish and English. The first English-language translation, *The Concept of Dread*, was by Walter Lowrie, published 100 years after *Begrebet Angest*. It was one of the last of Lowrie's twelve pathbreaking translations, all published within the amazingly short period of five years. Thirty-six years afterward came Reidar Thomte's translation (in collaboration with Albert B. Anderson) in the formidably annotated *Kierkegaard's Writings* edition, now as *The Concept of Anxiety*.

As *The Concept of Dread* this work had a troubled reception. Lowrie, Kierkegaard's dedicated salesman, admitted that "a great many parsons, especially in America, if they were to become acquainted with [Kierkegaard], would indignantly reject him."[2] Reviewers were by no means as inclined as Lowrie to embrace Kierkegaard. One reviewer, in the *American Journal of Sociology*, wrote that the "enthusiastic Kierkegaardians of our day do not, obviously, base their allegiance in [the] teachings of the master."[3] Another was even more dismissive, beginning with the words: "This book is interesting to the psychiatrist mainly because it inadvertently presents strong evidence that the writer is a psychiatric case."[4] To the extent that Kierkegaard might well agree, that of course is in fact a recommendation.

The two earlier translations differ considerably in style, the second extinguishing the energetic effusiveness which presented

Kierkegaard with a flourish that was in essence Lowrie's own, and keeping more faithfully to the sometimes epigrammatic perfunctoriness of much of the original. For etymological reasons, and because the work is now more familiar under that title, the new translation presented here retains "Anxiety" rather than "Dread." It helps also to make the link, or contrast, with psychiatric disorders with the same name (or "Angst") more evident. The tone of the original is preserved as far as possible while at the same time attention has been paid to making the translation read and sound as naturally in English as possible. Some restrictions have to be upheld in order not to lose too much of the measure of the original (Kierkegaard's Danish translates much more readily into German than into English). The widespread use of abstract nouns is a case in point. I have nevertheless tried to avoid and disambiguate the many occurrences of variants of the multipurpose "Bestemmelse" (in German "Bestimmung") usually translated as "determinant" and in related uses, as "qualified" and sometimes "category." Readers should note that the word "speculation" refers to either of two "home" disciplines within the tradition that has Absolute Spirit as its goal. These were respectively "speculative philosophy" and "speculative theology," the latter concerned with questions within "dogmatics," such as the role of revelation, and thus matters not embraced by Kierkegaard's psychology, while the former might include speculation about the status of dogmatics and the range of topics proper to it. Speculative philosophy is what Kierkegaard attacks.

Some politically sensitive readers may be disturbed by the occasional use of "man" as a translation of the genderless "Mennesket" (German *Mensch*). But to avoid the not altogether accurate rendering as "person" and the clumsiness of "human being," "man" occurs here in the relevant and easily identified standard English contexts. On the other hand, with the same sensitivity in mind, I have on occasion followed the Danish in treating "individual" (*Individet*) as a gender-neutral noun. As for "hereditary sin," this is preferred to "original sin" because it is closer to the Danish "Arvesynden," in which the notion of inheritance is explicit rather than implied.

Retranslators always have the advantage over their predecessors of being able to tackle the problems of translation in new ways. Unless very remiss they can also leave fewer literal mistakes. In some parts of the text it is hard to improve on Lowrie and also unwise to spend too much time trying. In several instances readers will find that both Thomte and I have either come to the same result or chosen to let Lowrie's version stand, particularly where Kierkegaard is at his most succinct. In translation there is no point in change for the sake of novelty. That these translations nevertheless differ overall, not just in detail but also in style, is as it should be. Multiple translation only goes to make it quite evident that any translation is nothing but a mock-up of the original, a reconcoction, and certainly not that impossibility, its reincarnation in an alternative language.

Up to the last moment Kierkegaard intended to publish *Begrebet Angest* under his own name. Why he changed his mind is not recorded, but a journal entry in connection with *Anxiety* from near the time of publication claims "a poetic relationship to my works, which is why I am a pseudonym."[5] The reason could be that he saw his writer's role as involving a kind of disengagement from his own person, which would of course justify almost any writer in adopting a pseudonym. But of all his pseudonyms, and just slightly behind *Either/Or*'s ironic "Victor Eremita" (Triumphant Recluse), *Anxiety*'s "Vigilius Haufniensis" (The Watchful Copenhagener) comes closest to describing Kierkegaard as he saw himself, as a rather special kind of writer, and one who, when later describing "how it went," said: "I presented the problem facing the whole human race: equality between man and man. I acted it out in Copenhagen. That is something else than writing a few words about it; I expressed it approximately with my life."[6]

The Concept of Anxiety is dedicated to Poul M. Møller, Kierkegaard's twenty-year-older friend and closest mentor who died six years before the work was published. A poet as well as philosopher, Møller had spent time as ship's chaplain on a China trader before becoming first a schoolteacher and then for two years professor of philosophy at the newly founded university in Oslo. He translated part of Homer's *Odyssey*, inspired Kierkegaard's interest in Socrates, and wrote commentaries on Aristotle. The expression "Joy over Denmark" is the title given to a poem Møller wrote while far from home on the China seas.

THE CONCEPT OF
ANXIETY

A Simple Psychologically Oriented
Deliberation in View of
the Dogmatic Problem
of Hereditary Sin

by

Vigilius Haufniensis

SECOND EDITION

The age of distinctions is past. It has been overcome by the system. Whoever loves them in our
day is considered an oddity whose soul clings to
something long since vanished. Be that as it may,
Socrates is still what he was, the simple wise
man, with the curious distinction that he himself expressed, both in words and in life, something that the singular Hamann first repeated
with great admiration 2,000 years later: "For
Socrates was great . . . in that he distinguished
between what he understood and what he did
not understand."

Preface[1]

As I see it, anyone wanting to write a book does well to think quite a lot on the subject he wants to write about. Nor does it do any harm to familiarize himself as much as possible with what has been written before on the same subject. If, in the course of this, he comes upon someone who has treated some area or other exhaustively, and to satisfaction, he does well to rejoice just like the bridegroom's friend when he stands and hears the bridegroom's voice.* Having done that, in all privacy, and with the fervor of love that always seeks out solitude, nothing more is needed. He should then write the book straight off as the bird sings its song. Should it benefit anyone, or bring them joy, so much the better; he should then publish it without care or concern, without any self-importance as though he had brought it all to a conclusion, or as if every family of the earth should be blessed in his book.† Every generation has its task and need not trouble

---

* [John 4:29]
† [Genesis 12:3]

itself all that unduly with being everything for those before and after. To each individual in the generation it is as if each day has its troubles,* as though shifting for oneself were enough, without any need to enclose the entire contemporary world in one's fatherly embrace, or have an era or an epoch begin with one's book, still less with the torch of one's New Year's resolution,² or the far-reaching promises of one's hints or reassuring references concerning a doubtful currency. Not everyone who is round-shouldered is therefore an Atlas, or has become so by carrying a world; not everyone who says "Lord, Lord" enters for that reason the kingdom of heaven;† not everyone who goes surety for the whole age proves by this that he can vouch for himself; not everyone who cries, "Bravo!" "Schwere Noth! [I'll be damned!]," "Gottblitz! [God help me!]," "Bravissimo!" has thereby understood himself and his wonderment.

As for my own humble person, I confess myself in all sincerity a king without a country but also, in fear and much trembling,‡ an author without pretensions. If a noble envy or jealous criticism thinks it too much that I bear a Latin appellation, I shall gladly assume the name Christen Madsen, preferring to be regarded as a layman who does indeed speculate but is far removed from speculation, even if in my unquestioning faith I am as devout as the Roman was tolerant about which God to worship. When it comes to human authority I am a fetish worshipper and will worship anyone with equal piety if only it becomes sufficiently clear, with the beating of drums, that this year it is him I am to worship,

* [Matthew 6:34]
† [Matthew 7:21]
‡ [1Corinthians 2:3]

that he is the authority and *Imprimatur*.[3] The decision is above my head, whether done by lottery or balloting, or the honor itself goes by rotation and the individual assumes authority like a citizens' representative on the board of arbitration.

I have nothing more to add except to wish anyone who shares my view and equally anyone who does not, anyone who reads the book and equally anyone for whom the preface was enough, a truly sincere "live well"!

COPENHAGEN

Respectfully
Vigilius Haufniensis

Contents

Introduction

In what sense the subject of this deliberation is a matter of psychological interest, and in what sense having interested psychology it points precisely in the direction of dogmatics.

That every scientific problem within the wide embrace of science has its appointed place, its aim and limit, and for just that reason its harmonious fusion within the whole, its justified consonance in what the whole tells us, this consideration is not merely a *pium desiderium* [pious wish] that ennobles the man of science with its inspiring or wistful fervor, not merely a sacred duty that binds him in service to the whole and bids him forsake anarchy and the adventurer's urge to lose sight of the land; it is also in the interest of every more specialized deliberation, because by forgetting where it belongs it also, as language with its well-aimed ambiguity is wont to put it, forgets itself, becomes something else, attains a suspect perfectibility in being able to become whatever it likes. Occasionally, by not being called to scientific order, and not seeing to it that the particular problems don't hurry past one another as though it were a matter of being first to arrive at a masked ball, one may achieve a certain brilliance, sometimes cause amazement through having already grasped what is far beyond one, sometimes be able with loose words to discover agreement in things that differ. Afterward, however, this profit brings upon itself its own revenge, like all illegal acquisition that cannot be brought under civic or scientific ownership.

Thus by captioning the last section of the *Logic* "Actuality" one gains the advantage of appearing to have reached the highest, or if you prefer, the lowest, through logic.[1] The loss is, however, obvious since neither logic nor actuality is served thereby: not actuality since contingency, an essential ingredient in actuality, is something that logic cannot let in; and no good is done to logic since if logic has thought actuality, it has ingested something it cannot assimilate, anticipated something for which it merely prepares the way [*prædisponere*]. The penalty is clear: every deliberation about what is actual is held back, yes, and perhaps for some time made impossible, since the word "actuality" must first be given time to as it were come to its senses, time to forget the mistake.

Similarly in dogmatics, to call *faith* the *immediate* with no more precise definition[2] gives one the advantage of convincing everyone of the necessity of not stopping with faith, yes, gains one even the concession of the orthodox on this point since perhaps the latter fails to see through the misunderstanding straightaway, that it is not due to what comes later but to this πρῶτον πσευδος [basic error]. There is no mistaking the loss, since faith loses through being deprived of what is lawfully its own: its historical presupposition. Dogmatics loses by having to start somewhere else than where it has its beginning, within an earlier beginning; instead of presupposing an earlier beginning, it ignores it and begins without further ado as if it were logic, for logic does indeed begin with the most elusive product of the finest abstraction: the immediate.[3] What is logically correct, namely, that the immediate is *eo ipso* [by that very fact] canceled, becomes in dogmatics mere chat; for it could occur to nobody to want to stay with the immediate (not further defined), seeing indeed that it is nullified the very moment it is mentioned, just as a sleepwalker wakes up the moment someone mentions his name.

Thus when, in the course of investigations that are little more than propaedeutic,[4] one sometimes finds the word "reconciliation" used to designate speculative knowledge, or the identity of the knowing subject and the thing known,[5] the subject-objective, etc., it is easy to see that the author is brilliant, and that with his brilliance he has explained all riddles, especially for those who in science do not take even the precaution they observe in everyday life of listening carefully to the words of the riddle before guessing it. Otherwise one acquires the incomparable merit of having, by way of this explanation, proposed a new riddle, namely, how it could occur to anyone that this might be the explanation. That thinking is, in general, in possession of reality was the assumption of all ancient philosophy, as well as of the philosophy of the Middle Ages. With Kant this assumption was put in doubt. Suppose now that the Hegelian school had really *thought through* Kant's skepticism[6] (though this may always remain a big question in spite of all Hegel and his school with the help of the catchphrase "Method and Manifestation" have done to hide what Schelling[7] owned to more revealingly with the catchphrase "intellectual intuition and construction," namely, that it was a new point of departure) and had reconstructed the earlier view in a higher form in which thought does not possess reality on the strength of a presupposition; is, then, this reality that is consciously brought about by thinking a reconciliation? Philosophy is simply brought

to the point where one began in the old days when reconciliation
had its enormous significance. We have an old and respectable
philosophical terminology: thesis, antithesis, synthesis.[8] A newer
one has been invented in which mediation takes third place. Is
this such an extraordinary step forward? Mediation is equivocal,
for it suggests simultaneously the relation that holds between the
two terms and also the result of the relation, that in which they
relate to each other as the terms that have come into that relation.
It describes movement but at the same time rest. Whether this
is a perfection only a far profounder dialectical test of mediation
will decide, but for that we are unfortunately still waiting. So they
do away with synthesis and say Mediation. So be it. But brilliance
demands more, so they say Reconciliation.

What follows from that? It does no good to their propaedeutic investigations, for these naturally profit just as little as truth
profits in clarity or a man's soul in blessedness through acquiring
a title. On the contrary, two sciences, ethics and dogmatics, are
fundamentally confused, particularly when having had the word
reconciliation brought in, they now point out that logic and λόγος
(the dogmatic) correspond and that logic is the proper doctrine of
λόγος.[*9] Ethics and dogmatics fight over reconciliation in a fateful
confinium [frontier zone].[10] Repentance and guilt extort reconciliation ethically, whereas dogmatics, in its willingness to accept the
proffered reconciliation, now has a historically concrete immediacy with which to begin its discourse in the great conversation of
science. What will follow now? Presumably language will come
to celebrate a great sabbatical year[†] in which speech and thought

[*] [John 1:1–2,14]
[†] [Leviticus 25:2–7]

take a rest so as to begin with the beginning. In logic *the nega-tive* is used as the quickening power that brings movement into everything. And movement one must have in whatever way one can, by fair means or foul. The negative helps, and if the negative cannot, then wordplay and platitudes can, just as the negative itself has become a play on words.* In logic, no movement may *come about*, for logic *is*, and everything logical simply *is*,† and this, logic's impotence, is logic's passing over into coming about, where human life [*Tilværelsen*] and actuality step forward. So when logic gets absorbed in the concretion of the categories, what was at the beginning remains constantly the same. In logic every movement, if for a moment we are to use that expression, is an

---

Exempli gratia: Wesen ist was ist gewesen, ist gewesen is a *tempus præteritum* of *seyn*, *ergo Wesen* is *das aufgehoben Seyn*, the *Seyn* that has been [e.g., Essence is what has been; "has been" is the past tense of "to be," *ergo*, essence is annulled being, being that has been]. This is a log-ical movement! If anyone were to take the trouble in the Hegelian Logic (in itself and with the contributions of the School) to pick out and assemble all the strange pixies and goblins who, like hirelings, help the logical movement along, a later age would perhaps be astonished to dis-cover that witticisms long considered discarded once played a great role in logic, not as incidental explanations and clever observations, but as masters of movement that made Hegel's logic a marvel and gave logical thought feet to walk on, though without anybody noticing, since amaze-ment's long cloak hid the trolley, just as Lulu [in a romantic opera where a character is transformed into a dwarf] comes running without anyone seeing the machine. Movement in logic, this is Hegel's merit, compared with which it is hardly worth mentioning the unforgettable merit that is his, and that he has turned down in order to run aimlessly [1 Cor. 9:26], for having in manifold ways enriched the categorial definitions and their arrangement.

†Logic's eternal expression is what the Eleatic [pre-Socratic fifth-century BC] School [founded by Parmenides in Elea] transferred through a misunderstanding to existence: nothing arises, everything is.

immanent movement, which in a deeper sense is no movement, as one will easily convince oneself by reflecting that the very concept of movement is a transcendence that can find no place in logic. The negative, then, is the immanence of movement, it is the vanishing factor, what is annulled.[11] If everything happens in this way, then nothing happens at all and the negative becomes a phantom. But precisely in order to get something to happen in logic, the negative becomes something more; it becomes what produces opposition and not a negation but a contraposition. The negative is then not the muteness of the immanent movement, it is the *"necessary other,"*[12] which may no doubt be most necessary for logic in order to set things going, but which the negative is not. If we leave logic and proceed to ethics, here again as in the whole Hegelian philosophy we find the negative indefatigably active. To our amazement, we find that the negative here is the evil. Confusion is now in full swing, there are no bounds to brilliancy, and what Mme. de Staël-Holstein[13] has said of Schelling's philosophy, that it makes a person clever for a lifetime, is true in every way of the Hegelian. One sees how illogical the movements in logic must be, since the negative is the evil, and how unethical they must be in ethics, since the evil is the negative. In logic it is too much, in ethics too little. If it has to fit both places, it fits nowhere. If ethics has no other transcendence, it is essentially logic; if logic is to have as much transcendence as ethics requires to preserve common decency, then it is no longer logic.

What is expounded here is perhaps rather elaborate for its place (though in relation to the subject it deals with it is very far from too long), but it is by no means extraneous since the detail is chosen in allusion to this work's topic. The examples are from the larger world, but what occurs in the larger must repeat itself in the smaller, and the misunderstanding is similar even if the result-ing harm is less. He who sets himself up as a writer of the Sys-tem[14] has his responsibility in the large things, but he who writes a monograph can be, and ought to be, trustworthy in the small.*

The present work has set itself the task of treating "anxiety" psychologically in such a way as to have in mind and view the dogma of hereditary sin. Accordingly, it has to take account, although tacitly, of the concept of sin. Sin, however, is no matter for psychological concern, and it would only be to abandon oneself to the service of a misunderstood cleverness if one were to treat it so. Sin has its definite place, or rather it has none at all, but that is its characteristic. Treating it in another place, through framing it in a nonessential refraction in reflection, is to corrupt it. Its con-cept is then corrupted, and at the same time the mood properly corresponding to the correct concept† disturbed; instead of the genuine mood's perseverance we have the false moods' short-lived antics.[15] Accordingly, when sin is drawn into aesthetics, the mood becomes either frivolous or melancholic, for the category under which sin lies is contradiction and this is either comic or tragic. The mood is thus corrupted, since that corresponding to sin is

---

* [Matthew 25:21–23]

† The fact that science too, as much as poetry and art, assumes a mood on the parts of both producer and recipient, that an error in modulation is just as disturbing as an error in the exposition of thought, has been entirely forgotten in our age, when people have altogether forgotten inwardness and how to define appropriation in their joy at all the mag-nificence they thought to possess, or through greed lost like the dog which preferred the shadow [a story from the fabulist Phaedrus (c. 15 BC to AD 50), who borrowed from Aesop]. However, every error begets its own enemy. An error of thought has dialectics outside; the absence of mood or its falsification has the comical outside, as its enemy.

earnestness. Its concept is also corrupted, for whether it becomes comic or tragic it becomes something that subsists, or something inessential that is nullified, whereas sin according to its concept is to be overcome. The comic and the tragic in a deeper sense have no enemy but either a bogeyman to weep at or a bogeyman to laugh at.

If sin is dealt with in metaphysics, the mood becomes that of a dialectical parity and disinterest which weighs up sin as something that cannot stand up to thought. The concept is corrupted, for it is true indeed that sin is to be overcome, not however as something to which thought cannot give life, but as that which is there and as such each person's concern.

If sin is dealt with in psychology, the mood becomes that of the persistent observer, of the dauntless spy, not of the victorious flight of earnest out of it. The concept becomes another one, for sin becomes a state but sin is no state. Its idea is that of the continual nullifying of its concept. As a state (*de potentia* [potentially]) it *is* not, whereas *de actu* or *in actu* [actually] it is, and is again and again. The mood of psychology would be an antipathetic curiosity, but the right mood is earnest's stout-hearted resistance. Psychology's own mood is the anxiety of finding out, and in its anxiety it delineates sin while being alarmed again and again by the sketch it itself produces. When dealt with in this way, sin becomes the stronger, for properly speaking psychology relates to it in a feminine way. There is certainly an element of truth in this state of mind, and it no doubt emerges more or less in every person's life before the ethical appears; yet with such treatment sin does not become what it is, but a more or less.

So, as soon as one sees the problem of sin being dealt with, from the mood it is possible straightaway to see whether the concept is the right one. Whenever, for instance, sin is talked about as a sickness, an abnormality, a poison, a disharmony, the concept is being falsified.

Properly speaking, sin belongs in no science. It is a theme for the sermon, where the individual talks as an individual to the individual. In our own age, scientific self-importance has fooled the priests into becoming a kind of professorial deacon who also serves science and thinks preaching beneath his dignity. So no wonder preaching has come to be regarded as a very poor art. It is, however, the most difficult of all arts, and is in fact the art extolled by Socrates, that of being able to converse. Of course it does not follow that there has to be someone in the congregation who answers, or that it might help always to have someone brought in to respond. What Socrates really criticized the Sophists for, when distinguishing between their ability to speak but not converse, was that they were able to say a great deal about everything but lacked the element of appropriation. Appropriation is precisely conversation's secret.

To the concept of sin corresponds the mood of earnest. The science in which sin might most plausibly find a place would surely be ethics. However, there is a great difficulty here. Ethics is still an "ideal" science, but not only in the sense that every other science is ideal [involves forming abstract concepts]; it wants to bring ideality into actuality. On the other hand its movement is not that of raising up actuality into ideality.* Ethics points to ide-

---

* Closer consideration of this provides ample opportunity to realize how brilliant it was to caption the last section of *Logic* "Actuality," seeing that not even ethics gets that far. The actuality with which logic ends means, therefore, in regard to actuality, no more than the "being" with which it begins.

ality as a task and assumes that a person is in possession of the required conditions. Ethics unfolds a contradiction here precisely in making clear the difficulty and the impossibility. What is said of the law is true also of ethics, that it is a disciplinarian who in making a demand merely judges and does not beget.* Only Greek ethics was an exception, due to its not being ethics in the proper sense but retaining an aesthetic element. This is shown clearly in its definition of virtue, and in what Aristotle says often but also affirms in *Ethica Nicomachea* with charming Greek naïveté, that virtue by itself does not after all make a person happy and content; he must have health, friends, and earthly goods, and be happy in his family.[16] The more ideal ethics is, the better. It must not let itself be put off by the babble that it is no use asking the impossible; for even listening to such talk is unethical, is something for which ethics has neither *time* nor *opportunity*. Ethics has nothing to do with haggling, nor is this the way to reach actuality. If that is to be reached, the whole movement must be reversed. This feature of ethics, namely, its being ideal in this way, is what tempts one to employ now metaphysical, now aesthetical, now psychological categories in treating it. But of course ethics, above all sciences, must resist temptations, and for that reason too it is impossible for anyone to write an ethics without having entirely different categories up his sleeve.

Sin belongs then to ethics only because it is upon this concept that with the help of repentance it runs aground.† If ethics is to

---

* [Galatians 3:24]

† Several observations on this point are to be found in Johannes de Silentio's *Fear and Trembling* (Copenhagen 1843). The author several times lets the wishful ideality of the aesthetical run aground on the ideality required by the ethical, in order through these collisions to

allow the religious ideality to come in view, which is precisely that of actuality and is therefore just as desirable as that of aesthetics, and not impossible like that of ethics, and bring it to view in such a way that it emerges in the dialectical leap and with the positive mood, "See, everything has become new!" [2 Cor. 5:17] and in the negative mood which is the passion of the absurd, to which the concept of "repetition" corresponds. Either the whole of human existence [*Tilværelsen*] terminates in what the ethical requires or the condition is provided [cf. *Philosophical Crumbs*, 1844, SKS 4, 224–226] and, with it, all of life and existence begin afresh, not through an immanent continuity with the foregoing (which is a contradiction), but by a transcendence that separates the repetition from the first existence by a chasm such that it is only a figure of speech to say that the foregoing and the subsequent state are related to one another as the totality of the living creatures in the ocean are related to those in the air and on the land, although according to the opinion of some natural scientists that prototype is supposed to prefigure in its imperfection everything revealed in the latter. Regarding this category one may compare *Repetition* by Constantin Constantius (Copenhagen 1843). This is in fact a whimsical book, as its author meant it to be, but it is nevertheless, so far as I know, the first to have grasped repetition energetically and to bring out the concept's pregnance with sufficient clarity to throw light on the relation between the pagan and the Christian, by pointing to the invisible summit and the *discrimen rerum* [turning point] where science breaks against science until the new science comes forth. But what he has discovered he has hidden again by arraying the concept in the jest of an analogous notion. What has moved him to do this is hard to say, or rather difficult to understand; for he says himself that he writes this "in such a way that the heretics would not understand him." [*Repetition*, in Repetition *and* Philosophical Crumbs, trans. Piety, p. 76]. Since he has wanted to occupy himself with this subject only aesthetically and psychologically, everything has had to be planned humoristically, and the effect thus brought about of the word at one moment signifying everything and at the next moment the most trivial thing of all, and the transition, or rather the perpetual falling down from the clouds, is justified by its burlesque contrast. But he has stated the whole thing pretty clearly on page 34: "Repetition is the *interest* of metaphysics, and also the interest upon which metaphysics becomes stranded. Repetition is the solution [*Løsnet*—also: catchword] in every ethical contemplation.

Repetition is the *conditio sine qua non* [the indispensable condition] for every dogmatic problem" [Piety, trans., p. 19]. The first sentence alludes to the proposition that metaphysics is disinterested, just as Kant affirmed of ethics. As soon as interest emerges, metaphysics steps aside. That is why the word "interest" is italicized. In actuality, all the interest of subjectivity comes in and then metaphysics runs aground. If repetition is not posited, ethics becomes a binding power. Presumably it is for this reason that he says that "it is the solution in every ethical view." If repetition is not posited, dogmatics just cannot exist since repetition begins in faith, and faith is the organ for the problems of dogmatics.—In the realm of nature, repetition is in its unshaken necessity. In the sphere of spirit, the task is not to exact change from repetition and during repetition to feel relatively comfortable, as if spirit stood in only an external relation to the repetitions of the spirit (in consequence of which good and evil alternate like summer and winter); the task is to transform repetition into something inward, into freedom's own task, into freedom's highest interest as to whether it really can, while everything changes, realize repetition. At this point the finite spirit despairs. Constantin Constantius has intimated this by stepping aside and letting repetition emerge in the young man on the strength of the religious. That is why Constantin says several times that repetition is a religious category, too transcendent for him, the movement on the strength of the absurd, and on page 142 [Piety, trans., p. 75] it is further said that eternity is the true repetition. All of this Professor Heiberg has failed to observe but, with his knowledge (which like his *New Year's Gift* is singularly elegant and tidy), has been kindly willing to help it become a tasteful and elegant triviality by bringing the question, with great pomposity, to the point where Constantin begins, to bring it to where (to recall a recent book) the aesthetic writer in *Either/Or* had brought it in "Crop Rotation." If Constantin should really feel flattered to savor the rare honor that brings him into an undeniably elect company in this way, then to my way of thinking, since it was he who wrote the book, he must have become, as one says, raving mad. If, on the other hand, an author like him who writes in order to be misunderstood were to forget himself and had too little ataraxia [peace of mind] to account it to his credit that Professor Heiberg had not understood him—then again he must be raving mad. This I have no need to fear, for the fact that up to now he has not replied to Professor Heiberg indicates sufficiently that he has understood himself.

include sin, its ideality is at an end. The more it remains in its
ideality, without ever becoming inhuman enough to lose sight of
actuality, but in correspondence with it by being willing to submit
itself as a task for everyone in such a way as to make each person
the true human being, the whole human being, the human being
κατ' ἐξοχήν [in an eminent sense], the more it intensifies the difficulty. In the struggle to realize the task of ethics, sin appears
not as something that belongs only by chance to a chance individual; it pulls itself back ever more deeply as an increasingly more
profound presupposition, as a presupposition that goes beyond
the individual. Now everything is lost for ethics, and ethics has
helped in the losing of everything. A category has come to light
that lies entirely outside its scope. *Hereditary sin* makes everything still more desperate, that is, it removes the difficulty, not
however with the help of ethics but with that of *dogmatics*. As all
ancient thought and speculation were founded upon the assumption that thought is in possession of reality, so also was all ancient
ethics based upon the assumption that virtue is realizable. Sin's
skepticism is altogether foreign to paganism. For the ethical consciousness sin is what error is with regard to knowledge: the particular exception that proves nothing.

   With dogmatics begins the science which, in contrast to that
ideal science strictly so called, begins with actuality. It begins
with the actual in order to raise it up into ideality. It does not deny
the presence of sin; on the contrary it assumes it and explains it
by presupposing hereditary sin. However, since dogmatics is very
seldom dealt with in its purity, hereditary sin will often be found
to have been brought within its bounds in a way that prevents the
heterogeneous primitivity of dogmatics from leaping to the eye
and obscures that impression, as also happens when one finds in

it a dogma about angels, about the Holy Scripture, etc. Hereditary sin is therefore not to be explained by dogmatics; the explanation is that it is something presupposed, like that vortex that the Greek speculation about nature talked so much about, a moving something which no science can get a hold of.[17]

That such is the case with dogmatics will be readily admitted if time is taken once more to understand Schleiermacher's immortal service to this science.[18] He was abandoned long ago when they chose Hegel; and yet Schleiermacher was a thinker in the beautiful Greek sense who could talk of what he knew, whereas Hegel, in spite of his remarkable ability and colossal learning, nevertheless reminds us again and again by his performance that he was in the German sense a professor of philosophy on a large scale, who must *à tout prix* [at all costs] explain everything.

So the new science begins with dogmatics in the same way that science of the immanent begins with metaphysics. Here ethics finds its place again as the science that has the dogmatic consciousness of actuality as a task for actuality. This ethics does not ignore sin, and its ideality consists not in making demands ideally but in a penetrating consciousness of actuality, of the actuality of sin, yet not, be it noted, with metaphysical irresponsibility or psychological concupiscence.[19]

The difference in the movement is easy to see, also that the ethics of which we are now speaking belongs in another order. The first ethics ran aground on the sinfulness of the individual. So far from being able to explain this, the difficulty had to become still greater and ethically more enigmatic, in that the sin of the individual expanded to become the sin of the whole race.*

* [Romans 5:12]

Now came dogmatics and lent a hand with hereditary sin. The new ethics presupposes dogmatics and along with it, hereditary sin, and now, with that, explains the sin of the individual while at the same time presenting ideality as a task, not however by a movement downward from above, but upward from below.

Aristotle, as we know, used the name πρωτη φίλοσοφία [the first philosophy][20] to denote more especially metaphysics, although he included also a part of what to our notion belongs to theology. That in paganism theology should be treated there is entirely as it should be; it is the same lack of infinite reflection that made the theater, in effect, a kind of divine worship. Through abstracting from this ambiguity, we might retain this name and understand by πρωτη φίλοσοφία* the totality of science. We might call it pagan, its nature being that of immanence, or use the Greek term "recollection," and understand by *secunda philosophia* that whose nature is transcendence or repetition.†

The concept of sin does not then properly belong in any science; only the second ethics can deal with its manifestation, though not with its coming to be. For any other science to deal

---

*Schelling recalled [in the then still unpublished 1841–42 Berlin lectures that Kierkegaard had attended] this Aristotelian term to serve his distinction between negative and positive philosophy. By negative philosophy he understood "logic." That was clear enough. What was less clear to me, however, was what he really understood by positive, beyond it being clear that positive philosophy was what he wished to provide. However, having nothing to go on except my own interpretation, there is no point in going into this.

†Constantin Constantius has reminded us of this by pointing out that immanence runs aground upon "interest." It is only with this concept that actuality comes genuinely into view.

with it is to confuse the concept. Coming closer to our theme, this would be the case if psychology were to do so.

What psychology deals with must be something resting, something that remains in agitated repose, not something restless that is constantly reproducing itself or being repressed. But the abiding state out of which sin constantly comes into being, not by necessity, for a becoming by necessity is simply a state of being (as for example the entire history of the plant), but by freedom—this abiding state, this predisposing assumption, sin's real possibility, this is an object of interest for psychology. What can occupy psychology, and what it can occupy itself with, is how sin can come to be, not *that* it comes to be. It can, in its psychological interest, bring things to the point of sin seeming to be there; but the next step, the fact that it is there, differs qualitatively from this. How this presupposition for psychology's painstaking contemplation appears ever expansively, this is what interests psychology. Yes, psychology wants as if to abandon itself to the illusion that sin is there. But this latter illusion is psychology's impotence and shows that it has served its turn.

That human nature must be so constituted as to make sin possible is, psychologically speaking, quite true; but to want to have this possibility of sin become its actuality is upsetting for ethics, and to dogmatics it sounds like blasphemy; for freedom is never possible; as soon as it is, it is actual in the same sense in which an earlier philosophy has said that if God's existence is possible, then it is necessary.[21]

As soon as sin is actually posited, ethics is on the spot and now follows every step it takes. How it came into being does not concern ethics, except insofar as it is certain that sin came into the world as sin. But still less than any concern with the genesis of sin is ethics concerned with the still life of its possibility.

If one now asks more specifically in what sense, and to what extent, psychology pursues its object of observation, it is clear from the foregoing, as in itself, that every observation of the actuality of sin as an object of thought is irrelevant to it, and nor as an object of observation does it belong to ethics, for the latter is never observing, but accusing, judging, acting. It follows furthermore from the foregoing, as is evident in itself, that psychology is not concerned empirically with the actual detail assigned to it except insofar as this lies outside sin. As a science, indeed, psychology cannot have anything to do empirically with the detail assigned to it, and yet this detail may receive its scientific representation the more concrete psychology becomes. In our times, this science, which is after all allowed above all others to just about intoxicate itself in the spuming manifold of life, has become as spare in its diet and as ascetic as any flagellant. This is not the fault of the science but of its devotees. With respect to sin, however, the whole content of actuality is properly denied to it; what belongs to it is only its possibility. To ethics, of course, the possibility of sin never occurs, and ethics does not let itself be fooled into wasting its time on such reflection. Psychology, on the other hand, loves it; it sits sketching the contours and calculating the angles of possibility and would, no more than Archimedes, let itself be disturbed.[22]

But while psychology thus delves into the possibility of sin, it is unawares in the service of another science which is only waiting for it to finish so as to begin and to help psychology in obtaining the explanation. This other science is not ethics, for ethics has nothing at all to do with this possibility. No, it is dogmatics, and here the problem of hereditary sin arises once more. While psychology fathoms the real possibility of sin, dogmatics explains hereditary sin, that is, the ideal possibility of sin. The second ethics has, on the other hand, nothing to do with sin's possibility or with hereditary sin. The first ethics ignores sin, the second ethics has the actuality of sin within its scope, and here again psychology can intrude only through a misunderstanding.

If what has been expounded here is correct, it is easy to see with what justification I have called this book a psychological deliberation, and also how this deliberation, insofar as it brings to consciousness its relation to science, belongs to psychology and points in turn toward dogmatics. Psychology has been called the doctrine of the subjective spirit. If we pursue this science a little more closely we will see how, when it comes to the problem of sin, it must first switch over to the doctrine of Absolute Spirit. There lies dogmatics. The first ethics presupposes metaphysics, the second ethics dogmatics, but it also completes it in such a way that, here as everywhere, the presupposition comes out.

This was the task of the introduction. The introduction may be correct—while the deliberation itself on the concept of anxiety may be entirely incorrect. Whether that is so remains to be seen.

I

Anxiety as Hereditary Sin's Presupposition
and as Clarifying Hereditary Sin
Retrogressively in Terms of its Origin

§1

Historical Hints Regarding the
Concept of Hereditary Sin

Is this concept identical with that of the first sin, Adam's sin, the fall of man? That is how people have sometimes taken it and accordingly set themselves the task of explaining the identity of hereditary sin with Adam's. When thought stumbled here on difficulties, they chose a way out. In order to have some kind of explanation they introduced a fanciful presupposition, the loss of which was the Fall. The advantage of this was that everyone freely admitted that the world contained no such condition as the one described, but it was forgotten that the doubt concerned something else, namely whether it had ever existed, that being rather necessary if it was to be lost. The history of the human race got a fanciful start, Adam was placed fancifully outside, pious feeling and fantasy got what they wanted, a godly prelude, but thinking got nothing. Adam was held fancifully out in two ways:

the presupposition was a piece of fanciful dialectic, especially in Catholicism (Adam lost *donum divinitus datum supranaturale et admirabile* [a supernatural and wonderful gift bestowed by God]), and it was a historical fantasy, particularly in the federal[1] theology that lost itself in the drama of Adam's appearance as proxy for the whole human race. Naturally, both explanations explain nothing. The one explains away its own poetic gloss; the other merely adds one that gives no explanation.

Does the way in which the concept of hereditary sin differs from that of the first sin mean that it is only through a relation to Adam that the individual participates in it, and not through its own primitive relation to sin? If so, then Adam is again taken fancifully out of history. His sin then becomes more than past (*plusquam perfectum* [pluperfect]). Hereditary sin is here and now, it is sinfulness and Adam is the only one in whom it was not, since it was through him that it came into being. No attempt was made to explain Adam's sin; what they wanted to explain was hereditary sin in what followed from it. The explanation was not however meant for thought. One can readily understand therefore that one of the symbolical scripts asserts the impossibility of an explanation, and that this assertion stands without contradicting the explanation. The *Smalcald Articles*[2] expressly teach: *Peccatum hæreditarium tam profunda et tetra est corruptio naturae, ut nullius hominis ratione intelligi possit, sed ex scripturae patefactione agnoscenda et credenda sit* [hereditary sin is so profound and detestable a corruption in human nature that it cannot be comprehended by human understanding, but must be known and believed from the revelation of the Scriptures].

This assertion is perfectly compatible with the explanations, for what comes out in these are less terms of reasoned thinking than the pious feeling (with an ethical intent) that vents its indignation over hereditary sin, takes on the role of accuser, and now, in something like a feminine passion and the intoxication of a girl in love, is concerned only with making sinfulness and its own participation in it more and more detestable, itself included, so that no word is harsh enough to describe the individual's participation.

If, bearing this in mind, we survey the various confessions, a gradation appears in which the profound piety of Protestantism wins the day. The Greek Church calls hereditary sin ἁμάρτημα προτοπατορικόν [the sin of the first father]. It lacks even a concept, since these words are in the form only of a historical statement, which unlike a concept applies not in the present but only to what has been carried to a historical conclusion. *Vitium originis* [the sin of the origin (i.e., the first sin)] (Tertullian)[3] is certainly a concept, but the form of the language allows the historical aspect to be grasped as the predominant one. *Peccatum originale* [original sin] (*quia originaliter tradatur* [because it has been transmitted from the origin], Augustine)[4] gives the concept, which is defined still more clearly through the distinction between *peccatum originans* and *originatum* [sin as a cause and as caused]. Protestantism rejects Scholastic definitions (*carentia imagines dei* [the absence of the image of God]); *defectus justitiae originalis* [loss of original righteousness]), just as it also rejects the notion that hereditary sin should be *poena* [punishment] (*concupiscentiam poenam esse non peccatum, disputant adversarii* [our adversaries contend that concupiscence is punishment and not a sin], *Apologia* A.C.).[5] And then begins the fervent climax: *vitium, peccatum, reatus, culpa* [vice, sin, guilt, transgression]. Since the concern is only with the contrite soul's eloquence, one occasionally comes on a quite contradictory thought (*nunc quoque afferens iram de iis, qui secundum exemplum* Adami *peccarunt* [which now brings the wrath of God upon those who have sinned following Adam's example]) in the discussion of hereditary sin. Or, a rhetorical concern that takes no consideration whatever of thought, but makes terrifying pronouncements about hereditary sin (*quo fit, ut omnes propter inobedientiam Adae et Hevae in odio apud deum simus*. Form. Conc. [from which it follows that all of us, because of Adam and Eve's disobedience, are hated by God—*Formula of Concord*],[6] which is nevertheless circumspect enough to protest against thinking it, otherwise sin would become man's substance).* Once the fervor of faith and contrition disappear, there can be no help from such definitions, since they only make it easy for wily matter-of-factness to wangle itself out of the acknowledgment of sin. To need other definitions is nevertheless a dubious proof of the perfection of our age, in just the same way as the need for other than Draconian laws.[7]

The same fanciful effect made evident here is repeated quite consistently at another point in dogmatics, in the Atonement. It is taught that Christ has rendered satisfaction for hereditary sin. But then what happens to Adam? After all it was he who brought hereditary sin into the world. So was hereditary sin not actual in him? Or does hereditary signify the same for Adam as for everyone in the human race? If that were so, the concept would be canceled. Or was Adam's whole life hereditary sin? Did the first sin not engender other sins in him, that is, actual sins? Here the fault in the foregoing becomes more evident; for Adam now finds himself so fancifully outside that he is the only one excluded from the Atonement.

No matter how one raises the problem, once Adam comes fan-

---

*That the *Formula of Concord* forbade thinking this concept is nevertheless to be praised precisely as proof of the energy of passion with which it could let thinking run up against the unthinkable, an energy much to be admired in contrast to modern thought, which is all too easygoing.

cifully outside, all is confused. To explain Adam's sin is therefore to explain hereditary sin. And no explanation that explains Adam but not hereditary sin, or explains hereditary sin but not Adam, is of any use. The deepest reason for this is, and what is essential to human existence, that the human being is *individuum* and, as such, at one and the same time itself and the whole human race, so that the whole race participates in the individual and the individual in the whole race.* Unless this is insisted on, one falls either into the Pelagian, Socinian, and philanthropic singular,[8] or else into fantasy. Prosaic common sense has it that the human race is numerically resolved into an *einmal ein* [one times one]. What is fanciful is that Adam should enjoy the well-intended honor of being more than the whole race, or the ambiguous honor of standing outside the race.

The fact is that the individual is at every moment itself and the race. This is the human being's perfection viewed as a state. It is at the same time a contradiction, but a contradiction always expresses a task, but a task is movement, but a movement toward that to which the task is directed is a historical movement. Hence the individual has a history. But if the individual has a history, then the race too has a history. Every individual has the same perfection; and for that very reason the individuals do not fall apart numerically, any more than the concept of the human race becomes a phantom. Every *individuum* is essentially interested in the history of all other individuals, yes, just as essentially as in its own. Perfection in oneself is therefore the perfect participation in the whole. No *individuum* is indifferent to the history of the human race, any more than is the race to that of any individual.

---

* For an individual to fall entirely out of the race would mean a modification of the race, whereas should an animal fall out of the species, the species would, on the contrary, be entirely unaffected.

Insofar as the history of the race advances, the individual begins constantly afresh, because it is itself and the race, and hence its history is, in turn, the history of the race.

Adam is the first human being; he is at once himself and the race. We do not stick to him on grounds of aesthetic beauty; it is not on the basis of a magnanimous sentiment that we attach ourselves to him, as though not to leave him in the lurch as the one who is to blame for everything; it is not by virtue of the fervor of sympathy and the persuasion of piety that we resolve to share guilt with him, as the child wants to share the guilt of the father; it is not on the strength of a forced compassion that teaches us to put up with whatever we must. It is on the strength of thought that we stick to him. Therefore every effort to explain Adam's significance for the race as *caput generis humani naturale, seminale, foederale* [head of the human race by nature, generation, covenant], to call the phrases of dogmatics to mind, confuses everything. He does not differ essentially from the race, for otherwise there is no race at all. He is not the race, for then too there would be no race. He is himself and the race. Whatever explains Adam therefore also explains the race, and vice versa.

§2

The Concept of the First Sin

According to traditional concepts, the difference between Adam's first sin and that of each person is this: As its condition, Adam's sin has sinfulness as consequence, the other first sin presupposes sinfulness as its condition. If this were so, Adam would really be outside the human race, and the latter would have begun not with him, but with a beginning outside itself, which is at odds with every concept.

That the *first* sin signifies something other than a sin (i.e., a sin like any other), something other than one sin (i.e., no. 1 in relation to no. 2), is easy to see. The first sin defines the quality, it is what sin is. This is the first sin's secret and its offense to abstract common sense, which thinks once is nothing but many times something, which is altogether preposterous since many times signifies either that each is just as much as the first or that, added together, they are not nearly as much. It is therefore a superstition in logic to think that in continuing a quantitative progression one adduces a new quality. It is an unpardonable reticence that makes no secret of the fact that things do not happen quite like that in the world, but then hides what follows from this fact for the whole of logical immanence by having it trickle into logical movement, as Hegel does.* The new quality appears with the first, with the leap, with the suddenness of the enigmatic.

If the first sin means numerically one sin, no history comes

---

*This proposition about the relation between quantitative definition and new quality has altogether a long history. Indeed all Greek sophistry simply consisted in affirming a quantitative definition, the height of difference hence lying in likeness and unlikeness. In modern philosophy Schelling first resorted to defining in purely quantitative terms in accounting for diversity, later blaming [Carl August von] Eschenmayer [(1768–1852), a German philosopher and physician] for doing the same (in his doctoral dissertation). Hegel laid down the leap [*Science of Logic*, vol. 1, bk. 1, §3, ch. 2] but in logic. Rosenkranz (in his *Psychology*) admires Hegel for this. In his latest publication (on Schelling), he reproves Schelling and praises Hegel. But Hegel's misfortune is precisely in his wanting to put the new quality into effect but then not wanting to do so, since he wants to do it in logic, which, once this is admitted, must acquire another awareness of itself and of its significance.

of it, and sin will then have no history, either in the individual or in the race. For they are both subject to the same condition, even though the history of the race is not that of the individual, any more than the history of the individual is that of the race, except insofar as the contradiction continually expresses the task.

It is through the first sin that sin came into the world. In exactly the same way this is true of each later person's first sin, that through it sin comes into the world. The fact that before Adam's first sin it was not to be found is itself, with regard to sin, a quite accidental and irrelevant consideration of absolutely no significance and which cannot justify making Adam's sin greater or every other person's sin less. Wanting to make it look as though sinfulness defined itself quantitatively in a person, until at last, through a *generatio aequivoca* [spontaneous generation], it produces the first sin in him, is indeed a logical and ethical heresy. This doesn't happen, any more than being a master in the service of doing sums would help Trop to attain a degree in jurisprudence.[9] Let mathematicians and astronomers help themselves out if they can with infinitely minute magnitudes; this does not help a person to obtain his examination papers in life itself, even less to explain spirit. If every subsequent person's first sin were brought about in this way by sinfulness, his first sin would be characterized as the first only in an inessential way, and have its essential character given—if such a thing is thinkable—by its serial number in the universal sinking fund of the race. But such is not the case, and it is equally foolish, illogical, unethical, un-Christian to court the honor of being the first inventor and then slink off by not putting any meaning into one's words, saying that one has only done what anyone else would do. The presence of sinfulness in a man, the power of the example, etc., all these are sheer quantitative attributes that explain nothing,* unless it is assumed that one individual is the race instead of that every individual is both itself and the race.

Especially in our day, the Genesis story of the first sin has in a rather offhand way been considered a myth. There is good reason for this, since what was put in its place was indeed a myth and a poor one at that, for when the understanding resorts to myth, what comes out of it is seldom more than prattle. That story is the only dialectically consistent account. Its whole substance is really concentrated in the statement: *Sin came into the world through a sin.* If that were not so, sin would have entered the world as something accidental, which one should no doubt refrain from explaining. The understanding's difficulty is precisely the triumph of the explanation, its profound consistency, namely that sin is its own presupposition, that its manner of coming into the world is to be presupposed in the fact that it is. Sin then comes into the world as the sudden, that is, through the leap. But this leap also posits the quality. But the very instant in which the quality is posited, the leap has turned into the quality and is presupposed by the quality and the quality by the leap. This is an offense to the understanding, *ergo* [therefore] it is a myth. By way of compensation understanding invents its own myth, which denies the leap and construes the circle as a straight line, and then everything goes along naturally. It talks fancifully about the human being's state prior to the Fall, and the projected innocence is little by little changed in the course of the chatting into sinfulness, and then—well then—there it is. Understanding's discourse can in

---

*What significance they otherwise have as belonging to the history of the human race, as run-ups to the leap, without being able to explain the leap, is another matter.

this event be conveniently compared with the counting rhyme in which children delight: one nis ball, two nis balls, etc., and so on until ten-nis balls. There it is, and arrived at quite naturally through what went before. If there were anything to the understanding's myth, it would be that sinfulness comes before sin. But if this is true, in the sense that sinfulness has entered through something other than sin, then the concept cancels out. But if it enters through sin, then sin comes first. This contradiction is the only dialectically consistent result that is equal to both the leap and immanence (i.e., the later immanence).

Through Adam's first sin *sin came accordingly into the world.* This statement, the common one, contains however an altogether external reflection that has without doubt contributed greatly to misty misunderstandings. That sin came into the world is quite true, but this is no concern of Adam's. To put it quite pointedly and accurately one must say: through the first sin, sinfulness entered Adam. It would not occur to us to say about any later person that it was through his sin that sinfulness came into the world; and yet it enters the world through him in a similar (i.e., not essentially different) way, because, put pointedly and accurately, sinfulness is in the world only insofar as it enters through sin.

That people have spoken in other ways about Adam is due solely to the consequence of Adam's fanciful relation to the human race having to manifest itself everywhere. His sin is hereditary sin. Apart from that, nothing is known about him. But hereditary sin seen in Adam is only that first sin. Is Adam then the only individual without a history? If so, the human race has its beginning with an individual that is not an individual, and the concepts of race and individual both thereby cancel out. If the history of any other individual in the human race can have significance in the history of the race, then Adam too has it. If Adam has it only by virtue of that first sin, then the concept of history cancels out, that is to say, history is over the moment it began.*

In view now of the fact that the human race does not begin over again with every individual,† the sinfulness of the race acquires a history. This however proceeds in quantitative terms, while it is in the leap of quality that the individual takes part in it. This is why the race does not begin anew with each individual, for otherwise there would be no race at all, but every individual begins anew with the race.

If it is now said that Adam's sin brought the sin of the race into the world, this is either meant fancifully, in which case every concept cancels out, or it can be said with equal justification of every individual who, by its own first sin, brings sinfulness into the world. To have the race begin with an individual standing outside the human race is as much a myth of the understanding as letting sinfulness begin in some other way than with sin. One contrives only to postpone the problem, which turns naturally to man no. 2 for the explanation or, more correctly, to man no. 1, since really man no. 1 has now become man no. 0.

What often deceives people and helps to set all sorts of fantasies in motion is the problem of the relation of generation, as though the subsequent person differed essentially from the first

---

*The problem is always to have Adam included in the race, and in exactly the same sense in which every other individual is included. This is something dogmatics should attend to, especially for the sake of the Atonement. The doctrine that Adam and Christ correspond to each other explains nothing at all and confuses everything. It may be an analogy but conceptually it is imperfect. Christ alone is an individual who is more than an individual, but for that reason neither does he come in the beginning, but in the fullness of time.

†The contrary is expressed in §1: as the history of the race proceeds, the individual continually begins anew.

by descent. Descent merely expresses the continuity in the history of the race, which always moves in quantitative terms and is therefore incapable of producing an individual, since an animal species, even if it has preserved itself through thousands of generations, never generates an individual. A second human being not descended from Adam would never have been the second human being but an empty repetition, out of which there became neither race nor individual. Every particular Adam would have become a statue on its own, and definable accordingly only by an indifferent property, that is, number, in an even more imperfect sense than when naming the "blue boys" by number.[10] At most, every single one would have been himself, not himself and the race, and never have acquired a history, just as an angel has no history but is only himself and does not take part in any history.

It need hardly be said that this view does not incur any Pelagianism, which lets every individual play his little history in his own private theater, unconcerned with the race. For the history of the race quietly pursues its course, and in this no individual begins at the same place as another, but every individual begins anew, and in the same instant he is at the place where he should begin in history.

§3

The Concept of Innocence

It is true, here as everywhere, that if one wants a dogmatic definition today, one must begin by forgetting what Hegel has come up with to help dogmatics. A strange uneasiness takes hold of one at this point when, in dogmatists who otherwise want to be somewhat orthodox, one finds Hegel's favorite remark to the effect that it is the nature of the immediate to be annulled, as though immediacy and innocence were altogether identical. Hegel has quite consistently dispersed every dogmatic concept just enough to support a reduced existence as a clever expression of the logical. That the immediate must be annulled we do not need Hegel to tell us, nor does he deserve immortal merit for having said it, since even in logical terms it is not correct; for the immediate, never having been [*da det aldrig er til*], is not to be annulled. The concept of immediacy belongs in logic, the concept of innocence in ethics, and every concept must be referred to in the terms of the science to which it belongs, whether the concept belongs to the science as one there to be explicated, or is explicated as a presupposition [of that science].

Now it is unethical to say that innocence must be annulled; for even if it were annulled in the instant of being uttered, ethics forbids us to forget that it can be annulled only through guilt. Therefore if one speaks of innocence as of immediacy, and has the logical impudence and bravado to treat this most fleeting of things as having vanished, or is aesthetically sensitive as to what it was and over its having vanished, then one is merely *geistrich* [clever] and forgets the point.

Just as Adam lost his innocence through guilt, so too does every human being. If it was not through guilt that he lost it, then it was not innocence that he lost, and if he was not innocent before becoming guilty, then he never became guilty.

As for Adam's innocence, there has been no shortage of all sorts of fanciful notions, whether these acquired a symbolic dignity in times when the velvet on the church pulpit was, as much as on the origin of the human race, less threadbare than now, or when they wandered at large, more romantically, like the suspect inventions of poetic fiction. The more fancifully Adam was arrayed, the more inexplicable it became that he could sin and the more appalling became the sin. He had, however, once and for all forfeited all the glory, and according to time and occasion one became sentimental or witty, melancholy or frivolous, historically contrite or whimsically cheerful. But one did not grasp the point of it ethically.

As for the innocence of those (i.e., all except Adam and Eve) who came after, here there were only some impoverished ideas. Ethical rigorism[11] overlooked the limit of the ethical and was righteous enough to believe that people would not make use of the opportunity to sneak away from it all when the escape was made so easy. Thoughtlessness grasped nothing at all. But only through guilt is innocence lost. Each loses innocence in essentially the same way that Adam lost it, and it is neither in the interest of ethics to make all of us except Adam into concerned and interested spectators of guiltiness but not guilty ourselves, nor in the interest of dogmatics to make all of us into interested and sympathetic spectators of the Atonement, but not ourselves expiated.

In wasting so much of the time of dogmatics and ethics, as well as one's own, in pondering what might have happened if Adam had not sinned, all it shows is that the right mood has not been brought along, nor consequently the right concept. It would never occur to the innocent person to ask such a question, but when the guilty person asks it, he sins, for he wants in his aesthetic curiosity to ignore the fact that he brought guilt into the world himself, and that he has lost his innocence through guilt.

Innocence is therefore not like the immediate, something that must be annulled, whose destiny it is to be annulled, something that is not really there but occurs only through being annulled, occurring as that which *was* before it was annulled and is now annulled. Immediacy is not annulled by mediacy, but when mediacy appears, it has in that same instant annulled immediacy. The annulment of immediacy is therefore an immanent movement within immediacy, or it is an immanent movement within mediacy in the opposite direction through which the latter presupposes immediacy. Innocence is something that is canceled by transcendence, just because innocence is *something* (whereas the most appropriate expression for immediacy is the one used by Hegel about pure being: it is nothing), which is also why, when innocence is canceled by transcendence, something quite different comes of it, while mediacy is precisely immediacy. Innocence is a quality, it is a *state* that may well endure, and therefore the logical haste to have it annulled has no point, whereas in logic itself it should try to hurry a little more, since there even at its quickest it always arrives too late. Innocence is not a perfection one should wish to regain, for as soon as one wants it, it is lost, and then to waste time on wishes is a new guilt. Innocence is not an imperfection in which one cannot remain standing, for it is always sufficient unto itself, and the person who has lost it in the only way it can be lost, that is, through guilt, and not in some way it might be pleasing to have lost it—to that person it could never occur to boast of perfection at the cost of innocence.

The Genesis story gives us now also the right explanation of innocence. Innocence is ignorance. It is by no means the pure being of the immediate, but it *is* ignorance. That ignorance, when viewed from outside, is seen in terms of knowledge is something that concerns ignorance not at all.

It is surely evident that this view does not incur a Pelagianism.

The race has its history. Within it, sinfulness has its continual quantitatively measurable identity, but innocence is always lost solely through the individual's qualitative leap. That this sinfulness, which is the progress of the human race, may appear as a greater or a lesser disposition in the particular individual who assumes it in its intention is indeed true, but this is a more or less, a quantitative identification which does not constitute the concept of guilt.

§4

The Concept of the Fall

If innocence then is ignorance, it seems that insofar as the guiltiness of the race in its quantitative identification is present in the ignorance of the individual, and that it is in the individual's intention that it manifests itself, then there must be a difference between Adam's innocence and that of each later person. The answer is already given, that a more does not constitute a quality. It may also seem easier to explain how a later person lost his innocence. This however is only appearance. The highest degree of quantifying modification no more explains the qualitative leap than does the lowest. If I can explain guilt in the later person, I can equally well explain it in Adam. Through habit, and even more through thoughtlessness and ethical stupidity, it has come to look as if the former were easier than the latter. One will so much rather avoid the sunray of consistency that aims straight at the crown of one's head. We would put up with sinfulness, go along with it, etc. We need not trouble ourselves, sinfulness is not an epidemic that spreads like foot-and-

mouth disease "and every mouth shall be silenced."* That a
person can say, in deep earnest, that he was born in misery† and
his mother conceived him in sin is quite true, but he can truly
sorrow over this only if he has brought guilt into the world and
brought all this upon himself; for it is a contradiction to want to
sorrow *aesthetically* over *sinfulness*. The only one who sorrowed
innocently over sinfulness was Christ, but he did not sorrow
over it as a fate that he had to put up with. He sorrowed as the
one who freely chose to bear all the world's sin and suffer its
punishment.‡ This is no aesthetic characterization, for Christ
was more than an individual.

So innocence is ignorance. But how is it lost? I do not mean
to repeat here all the ingenious and silly hypotheses with which
thinkers and crackpots, interested only out of curiosity in the great
human affair we call sin, have burdened the beginning of history,
partly because I do not want to waste others' time in recounting
what I myself wasted time in learning, and partly because the
whole thing lies outside history in that twilight where witches and
crackpots outdo one another on a broomstick and a nail.[12]

The science that has to do with the explanation is psychology,
which however can explain only as far as the explanation, and
must above all guard itself against appearing to explain what no
science explains and only ethics explains further by presupposing it through dogmatics. Taking the psychological explanation
and repeating it several times, and then thinking it not unlikely
that sin came into the world in this way, would be to confuse

* [Romans 3:19]
† [Psalms 51:5; the text has "guilty"]
‡ [Philippians 2:6–8; John 1:29]

everything. Psychology must keep within its bounds, and then its explanation can always have its significance.

A psychological explanation of the Fall can be found well and clearly presented in Usteri's exposition of the Pauline doctrines.[13] But theology has now become so speculative that it scorns such things, for it is after all much easier to explain that the immediate must be annulled, and what theology sometimes does is even more convenient: disappearing at the decisive moment before the eyes of its speculative devotees. Usteri's exposition amounts to saying that it was the prohibition itself not to eat of the tree of knowledge that gave birth to sin in Adam. This by no means ignores the ethical but allows that the prohibition in some way merely predisposes for what emerges in Adam's qualitative leap. But to propound this account as given any further is not my intention. Everyone has read it or can read it in the author's work.*

Where this explanation is lacking is in not wanting to be thoroughly psychological. It cannot be blamed for this, since that was not its intention, but rather the different task of developing the

---

*Anyone reflecting on this matter must of course know Franz Baader's [see note 6 to Chapter II] typically vigorous and authoritative presentation in several works on the meaning of temptation for the consolidation of freedom, and the misunderstanding of taking temptation one-sidedly to be temptation to evil, or as that which is destined to make man fall, when it should rather be regarded as freedom's necessary other. There is no need to repeat this here. Baader's works are extant. Nor is it possible to pursue his thought here, since it seems to me that Baader has overlooked the intermediate terms. The transition from innocence to guilt simply through the concept of temptation tends to bring God into what is almost an experimenting relation to man. It ignores the intermediate psychology, the middle term here being only *concupiscentia* [inordinate desire]. In short, his account is more a dialectical consideration of the concept of temptation than a psychological explanation of the detail.

doctrines of St. Paul and adhering to the Bible. But the Bible has often had a harmful effect in this way; one begins on a deliberation of this kind with certain classical passages fixed in mind, and the explanation then becomes no more than an arrangement of those passages, as if the whole thing were as extraneous as that. The more natural the better, even if one is willing with all deference to submit the explanation to a scriptural verdict, and if it fails the test, to try again. This at least prevents one from arriving at the preposterous position of having to understand the explanation before understanding what it is meant to explain, as well as the disingenuous position of using Bible texts in the way the Persian king, in resisting the Egyptians, used the latter's sacred animals to protect himself.[14]

Having the prohibition be the condition of the Fall assumes that the prohibition arouses concupiscence. Here psychology is already overstepping its bounds. A concupiscence is an attribute of guilt and sin prior to guilt and sin and yet is not guilt and sin, that is, posited through the latter. The qualitative leap is weakened, the Fall becomes something successive. Nor is it possible to grasp how the prohibition arouses concupiscence, however surely the human being's hankering toward the forbidden is shown both in pagan and Christian experience. But appeal cannot be made to experience in this way with no further ado, seeing that the further question must be asked as to in what segment of life this experience occurs. Nor is the middle term concupiscence ambiguous, from which it can be seen straightaway that this is no psychological explanation. The strongest, really the most positive, expression that the Protestant Church uses for the presence of hereditary sin in man is precisely that he is born with concupiscence (*Omnes homines secundum naturam propagati nascuntur cum peccato h. e. sine metu dei, sine fiducia erga deum et cum concupiscentia* [all men begotten in a natural way are born with sin, i.e., without fear of God, without trust in God, and with concupiscence]). Yet the Protestant doctrine makes an essential distinction between the innocence of the later person (if there can be any question of such) and the innocence of Adam.

The psychological explanation must not talk around the point but remain in its elastic ambiguity, from which guilt emerges in the qualitative leap.

§5

The Concept of Anxiety

Innocence is ignorance. In innocence the human being is not characterized as spirit but is psychically characterized in immediate unity with its natural condition. Spirit is dreaming in the human being. This view fully accords with that of the Bible which, by denying that the human being in its innocence has knowledge of the difference between good and evil,* condemns all Catholicism's fantasies concerning [Adam's] merit.[15]

In this state there is peace and repose, but at the same time there is something else, something that is not dissension and strife, for there is nothing against which to strive. What, then, is it? Nothing. But what effect does nothing have? It begets anxiety. This is the profound secret of innocence, that at the same time it is anxiety. Dreaming, spirit projects its own actuality, yet this actuality is nothing, but innocence always sees this nothing outside itself.

* [Genesis 3]

Anxiety is an attribute of the dreaming spirit and belongs as such to psychology. Awake, the difference between myself and my other [*mit Andet*]¹⁶ is posited; sleeping, it is suspended; dreaming, it is a nothing hinted at. Spirit's actuality appears constantly as a form that tempts its possibility but disappears as soon as it reaches out for it, and is a nothing that can only bring unease. More it cannot do as long as it merely appears. The concept of anxiety is hardly ever seen treated in psychology, so I must point out that it differs altogether from fear and similar concepts that refer to something definite; whereas anxiety is freedom's actuality as the possibility of possibility. For this reason anxiety will not be found in the beast,¹⁷ just because in its nature the beast does not possess the character of spirit.

When we consider the dialectical properties of anxiety, it appears that these possess precisely the ambiguity of the psychological. Anxiety is a *sympathetic antipathy* and an *antipathetic sympathy*. I think one readily sees that this is a psychological concept in a way quite other than the concupiscence of which we spoke. Linguistic usage confirms this perfectly. We speak of sweet anxiety, a sweet anxiousness; we speak of a strange anxiety, a shy anxiety, etc.¹⁸

The anxiety that is posited in innocence is, in the first place, not guilt and, in the second place, no heavy burden, not a suffering that cannot be brought into harmony with the blessedness of innocence. When we observe children, we find the anxiety more definitely intimated as a seeking after the adventurous, the prodigious, and the mysterious. That there are children in whom this anxiety is not to be found proves nothing, for neither does it exist in the beast, and the less spirit, the less anxiety. This anxiety belongs so essentially to the child that the child will not do without it;

although it alarms, in its sweet anxiousness it also captivates. In all peoples where the childlike is preserved as dreaming spirit, there is this anxiety. The profounder the anxiety, the profounder the people. Only a prosaic stupidity will think of it as a disorder. Anxiety has the same meaning here as melancholy at a much later point, where freedom, having passed through the imperfect forms of its history, will in the profoundest sense come to itself.*

Just as anxiety's relation to its object, to something, which is nothing (usage is also succinct here: to be anxious at nothing), is altogether ambiguous, so will the transition that can be made here from innocence to guilt be precisely so dialectical that it shows that the explanation is, as it must be, psychological. The qualitative leap is outside all ambiguity, but the person who becomes guilty through anxiety is indeed innocent, for it was not himself but anxiety, an alien power, that seized him, a power he did not love but about which he was anxious. And yet he is indeed guilty, for he sank down in anxiety, which he loved nevertheless in fearing it. Nothing in the world is more ambiguous than this; and that is why this is the only psychological explanation, even if, to repeat it once more, it would never take it into its head to want to explain the qualitative leap. Every notion of the prohibition having tempted him, or of the seducer having deceived him, has ambiguity enough only for a superficial observation; it distorts ethics, introduces quantitative terms and wants, with psychology's help, to pay humankind a compliment at the ethical's

---

* On this one may consult *Either/Or* (Copenhagen, 1843), especially if noting that in its anguished sympathy and egotism the first part is the melancholy that is explained in the second part.

expense, a compliment that anyone who is developed ethically must decline as a new, even profounder seduction.

Everything depends on anxiety coming into view. The human being is a synthesis of the psychical and the physical, but a synthesis is unthinkable if the two are not united in a third. This third is spirit. In innocence, the human being is not merely animal, for if at any moment in his life he were merely animal, he would never become a human being. So spirit is present but as immediate, as dreaming. So far as it is now present, it is in a sense a hostile power, for it constantly upsets the relation between soul and body, a relation that does have subsistence but then doesn't have it, because it receives it first through spirit. It is, on the other hand, a friendly power that wishes precisely to constitute the relation. What then is the human being's relation to this ambiguous power; how does spirit relate to itself and to that which conditions it? It relates as anxiety. To do away with itself, that spirit cannot do; seize itself, so long as it has itself outside itself, it cannot do that either. Nor can the human being sink down into the vegetative, for he is characterized as spirit. Flee from anxiety he cannot, for he loves it; really love it he cannot, for he flees from it. Innocence has now reached its peak. It is ignorance, not an animal brutishness but an ignorance characterized by spirit, and it is as such precisely anxiety, because its ignorance is about nothing. Here there is no knowledge of good and evil, etc., but the whole actuality of knowledge projects itself in anxiety as the enormous nothing of ignorance.

There is still innocence, but to focus the ignorance needs only a word. Ignorance, naturally, cannot understand this word, but anxiety has, as it were, caught its first prey. Instead of nothing it has an enigmatic word. Thus when, according to Genesis, God said to Adam "but of the tree of the knowledge of good and evil you shall not eat,"* Adam of course did not really understand these words, for how should he understand the difference between good and evil when this distinction only followed with the enjoyment?

To assume now that the prohibition awakens the desire† is to substitute knowledge for ignorance; for Adam would need to have had knowledge of freedom, since the desire was the desire to use it. This explanation therefore comes too late. The prohibition makes him anxious, because it awakens in him freedom's possibility. What innocence let slip as the nothing of anxiety now enters him, and here again it is a nothing—the anxious possibility of *being able*. What it is he is able to do, of this he has no idea, for if that were not so, that which comes later, the difference between good and evil, would be, as is commonly the case, presupposed. Only the possibility of being able is there, as a higher form of ignorance, as a higher expression of anxiety, because in a higher sense it both is and is not, because in a higher sense he both loves it and flees from it.

Following the word of prohibition comes the word of judgment: "Then you shall surely die."‡ Adam of course has no grasp at all of what it means to die, while on the other hand nothing prevents him, supposing that it was said to him, from acquiring a notion of the terrifying. In this respect, even the beast can under-

* [Genesis 2:16–17]
† [Romans 7:5,7]
‡ [Genesis 2:16–17]

stand the mimic expression and tremor in the voice of a speaker, yet without understanding the word.

Making the prohibition awaken the desire means also having the word of punishment awaken a notion of discouragement. But this confuses things. The terror here is simply anxiety, since Adam has not understood what was said, and so here again there is only the ambiguity of anxiety. The infinite possibility of "being able," which the prohibition awakened, now draws nearer through this possibility pointing to a possibility as its accompaniment.

Innocence is brought in this way to its extremity. In anxiety, it is related to the forbidden and to the punishment. It is not guilty, and yet there is an anxiety as though innocence were lost.

Further psychology cannot go, but this far it can reach and, above all, can demonstrate again and again in its observation of human life.

I have held to the biblical story here in this conclusion; I let the prohibition and the voice of punishment come from outside. This has naturally plagued many thinkers. But we need only smile at this difficulty. Innocence can after all speak. As for that, in language it possesses the expression for all that is spiritual. We need simply assume that Adam talked to himself. This eliminates the imperfection in the story, that another speaks to Adam about what he does not understand. From Adam's ability to talk, it does not follow that he was able in a deeper sense to understand what was said. This is true above all of the difference between good and evil, which is indeed made in language but nevertheless *is* only for freedom. Innocence can indeed give voice to this difference, but the difference is not one for innocence, and for innocence it has only the meaning we have indicated in the preceding account.

§6

Anxiety as Hereditary Sin's Presupposition and as Casting Light on Hereditary Sin Retrogressively in Terms of its Origin

Let us then look more closely at the Genesis account, trying to put aside the fixed idea that it is a myth, and reminding ourselves that no age has been as quick as our own to produce myths of the understanding, producing myths while wanting at the same time to eradicate all myth.

So Adam was created, had given names to the animals (there is a language here, though an imperfect one similar to that of children who learn by identifying animals by letters on an alphabet board), but had found no company for himself.* Eve was created, formed from his rib.† She stood in as intimate as possible a relation to him but still an external one; Adam and Eve are merely a numerical repetition.‡ Even a thousand Adams in this respect would mean no more than there being one. So much with regard to the descent of the race from one pair. Nature does not favor a meaningless superfluity, so if we assumed that the race descended from several pairs, a moment would come when nature had a meaningless superfluity. Once the relationship of generation is posited, no human being is superfluous, because every human being is itself and the race.

Now follow the prohibition and the judgment. But the serpent

---

*[Genesis 2:7, 18–20]
†[Genesis 2:21]
‡[Genesis 2:23]

was smarter than all the other wild animals, it enticed the woman.* Even if we call this a myth, it must not be forgotten that it in no way interferes with thought or confuses the concept, as does a myth of the understanding. The myth gives outward expression to something that is inward.

What we must note here to begin with is that the woman was seduced first, and that she then seduces the man. I shall try to explain in a later chapter in what sense woman is, as people say, the weaker sex, and that anxiety belongs to her more than to man.†

There have been several reminders in the preceding that the view presented in this work does not deny the propagation of sinfulness in generation, or in other words, that in generation sinfulness has its history. All that is said is that sinfulness moves in quantitative terms, while sin constantly enters through the individual's qualitative leap. Already here there is meaning to be seen in the generational quantifying. Eve is the one who is derived. True, like Adam she is created, but she is created out of a previous creature. True, like Adam she is innocent, but there is as though the hint of a disposition that, although not itself sinfulness, may appear as a presentiment of the sinfulness posited by propagation, which is derived, which predisposes the particular individual though without making the individual guilty.

Here we must be reminded of what was said in §5 about prohibition and the word of judgment. The imperfection in the nar-

---

* [Genesis 3:1–6]

† This has no bearing on woman's imperfection with respect to man. Although anxiety belongs to her more than to the man, anxiety is by no means a sign of imperfection. If we are to speak of imperfection, then it must be found in something else, that in anxiety she seeks beyond herself to another human being, to the man.

rative—how it could have occurred to anyone to say to Adam something that essentially he cannot understand—drops out if we bear in mind that what speaks is language, and also that it is Adam himself who speaks.*

There remains the serpent. I am no friend of cleverness and shall *deo volente* [God willing] resist the serpent's temptations, which have in the course of time, as at the beginning of time when it tempted Adam and Eve, tempted writers to be, well, yes, clever. I most freely admit to being unable to attach any definite thought to the serpent. The difficulty with the serpent is in any case something quite different, namely letting the temptation come from outside. This is directly opposed to the Bible's teaching, to that familiar classical passage in James which says that God tempts no one, and is not tempted by anyone, but each person is tempted by himself.† If one thinks to have rescued God by having man tempted by the serpent and thinks oneself so far in agreement with James "that God tempts no one," there is still the second statement to confront, that God is not tempted by anyone. For the serpent's attempt on man was also an indirect temptation of God through interfering with the relation between God and man; and one comes up against that third statement, that every man is tempted by himself.

---

*If one went on to say that there is then a question of how the first human being learned to speak, my answer would be that this is very true, but also that the question is beyond this entire investigation's scope. This must not, however, be understood in the manner of modern philosophy as though to suggest, in my evasive reply, that I *could* answer the question somewhere else. But this much is certain, that it will not do to have the human being itself as the inventor of language.

† [James 1:13–14]

There now follows the Fall.* This is something that psychology cannot explain, because the Fall is the qualitative leap. However, let us consider for a moment the outcome as presented in that story† so as to fasten our gaze once more upon anxiety as hereditary sin's presupposition.

The outcome was a double one, that sin entered the world and that sexuality was posited, and the one being inseparable from the other. This is of the utmost importance for showing humankind's original state. If man were not a synthesis that rested in a third, then one thing could not have had two outcomes. If man were not a synthesis of soul and body sustained by spirit, the sexual could never have entered with sinfulness.

Leaving pointless speculations aside, we simply assume sexual differentiation before the Fall, except that it wasn't really there, since in ignorance it *is* not. In this we have support in the Scriptures.‡

In innocence, Adam, as spirit, was dreaming spirit. The synthesis is thus not actual, for the combining factor is precisely spirit, and this is not as yet posited as spirit. In animals the sexual difference can develop instinctively, but that cannot be the case with the human being, just because the human being is a synthesis. The moment that spirit posits itself, it posits the synthesis; but in order to posit the synthesis it must pervade it differentially and the extremity of the sensuous is precisely the sexual. The human being can reach this point only in the instant that spirit becomes actual. Before that time, the human being is not ani-

---

* [Genesis 1:3]
† [Genesis 3:7–13]
‡ [Cf. Genesis 2:25]

mal but neither is it really man. The moment it becomes man, it becomes so by being animal as well.

Sinfulness is then not sensuousness, not at all; but without sin, no sensuousness and without sexuality, no history. A perfect spirit has neither the one nor the other, which is indeed why the sexual difference is canceled in the resurrection, and why no angel has a history either. Even if Michael had noted down all the missions upon which he had been sent and had accomplished, that is still not his history.[19] It is only in the sexual that the synthesis is posited as a contradiction, but also, as with every contradiction, as a task the history of which begins at that same instant. This is the actuality that freedom's possibility precedes. But freedom's possibility is not the ability to choose the good or the evil. Such thoughtlessness has as little to do with the Scriptures as with thought. The possibility is to *be able*. It is simple enough in a logical system to say that possibility passes over into actuality. In actuality itself it is less easy and an intermediate term is required. This intermediate term is anxiety, which no more explains the qualitative leap than it can justify it ethically. Anxiety is not a category of necessity, but neither is it a category of freedom; it is a hobbled freedom where freedom is not free in itself but tethered, not in necessity but in itself. If sin has entered the world by necessity (which is a contradiction) there can be no anxiety. If sin has entered through an abstract *liberum arbitrium* [free will] (which existed no more in the world in the beginning than it did later, since it is a conceptual monstrosity), then there is no anxiety either. To want to give a logical explanation of sin's entry into the world is a foolishness that can only occur to people who are comically anxious to find an explanation.

Were I granted a wish here, I would wish that no reader be so profound as to ask: What if Adam had not sinned? The moment actuality is posited, possibility walks by its side as a nothing that tempts all thoughtless persons. If only science could make up its mind to keep people in check and to rein itself in! When someone asks a foolish question it is better not to answer, otherwise one becomes as foolish as the questioner. The folly of that question consists not so much in the question as in its being directed at science. If one stays at home with it and, like Clever Else[20] with her projects, calls together like-minded friends, then one has at least understood, more or less, one's own stupidity. Science, on the other hand, cannot explain such things. Every science lies either in a logical immanence or in this immanence within a transcendence that it cannot explain. Now sin is precisely that transcendence, that *discrimen rerum* [critical point], in which sin enters the single individual as the single individual. Sin never enters the world otherwise; nor has it ever done so. So when the single individual is foolish enough to inquire about sin as if it were not the individual's concern, he asks as a fool, for either he has no idea of what the question is about and so cannot possibly acquire it, or he knows and understands the question and also knows that no science can give him the explanation.

Science has, on the other hand, been at times compliant enough in responding to sentimental wishes with deeply pondered hypotheses, which it then finally admits fail to provide adequate explanations. Which is also of course entirely true, but the confusion lies in science's not energetically dismissing foolish questions instead, on the contrary, of confirming, superstitious people in their notion that one day a scientific theory-monger would come along who was man enough to hit on the right answer. That sin came into the world 6,000 years ago is said in just the same tone of voice as one might say about Nebuchadnezzar that it was 4,000 years ago that he became an ox.* When the matter is understood in this way, it is not to be wondered at that the explanation fits. What is in one respect the simplest thing in the world has been made into the most difficult. What the most simpleminded person understands in his own way, and quite rightly so because he understands that it is not exactly 6,000 years since sin came into the world, science has with the theory-monger's art proclaimed as a prize problem still to be satisfactorily answered. How sin came into the world each person understands solely by himself. If he wants to learn it from someone else he *eo ipso* [by that very fact] misunderstands. The only science that can do a little is psychology; yet it admits that it does not explain more, that it *cannot* and *will not*. If any science were able to explain it, everything is confused. That the scientist is said to forget himself is quite true; but then how fortunate it is that sin is no scientific problem, so that no man of science, any more than any theory-monger, is obliged to forget how sin entered the world. If he wanted to do that, if he magnanimously wanted to forget himself, he would in his enthusiasm to explain all of humanity become as comical as that privy councilor who was so conscientious about parting with his calling card to every Tom, Dick, and Harry that in doing so he finally forgot his own name. Or his philosophical enthusiasm will make him so absentminded that he needs a good-natured, level-headed wife, whom he can ask, as Soldin asked Rebecca, when in enthusiastic absentmindedness he too lost himself in the objectivity of chatter: "Rebecca, is it I who am speaking?"[21]

  That my much honored age's admired men of science, men

---

* [Daniel 4:25–31; "made to eat grass like oxen"]

who in their concern for the system, and in their search for it, a concern known to the whole congregation and no doubt includes finding a place within it for sin, may find all this highly unscientific is quite as it should be. But let the congregation join in the search, or at least include these profound seekers in their pious intercessions; they will find the place as surely as one who hunts the thimble and in getting warmer and warmer finds it, not realizing it has been burning in his own hand.

II

—

Anxiety as Hereditary Sin Progressively

With sinfulness sexuality was posited. At that very moment begins the history of the human race. Just as sinfulness in the race moves in quantitative categories, so too does anxiety. The outcome of hereditary sin, or hereditary sin's presence in the individual, is anxiety, which differs only quantitatively from that of Adam. In the state of innocence—and it must be possible to talk of such a thing in the later human being—hereditary sin must have that dialectical ambiguity out of which guilt emerges in the qualitative leap. Anxiety in the later individual will, on the other hand, be better able to reflect itself than in Adam, because in the later individual the quantitative accumulation that the race puts behind it now takes effect. As little as ever, however, will anxiety here be an imperfection in the human being; on the contrary, one has to say that the more pristine the human being, the deeper the anxiety, because the presupposition of sinfulness that the individual life takes upon itself on entering the history of the race has to be made its own. Sinfulness has in this way acquired a greater power, and hereditary sin is growing. That there are some who notice no anxiety at all may be understood in the way Adam would have experienced none had he simply been an animal.

The later individual is, like Adam, a synthesis sustained by spirit; but the synthesis is one that is derived, and the history of the race is to that extent posited in it. Here is where the more or less of anxiety lies in the later individual. As yet this anxiety is nevertheless not an anxiety about sin, since there is no distinction between good and evil, that distinction coming only through the actuality of freedom. If present, it is there only as an intimated idea, which, again, through the history of the race can mean a more or less.

That anxiety in a later individual is more reflected due to participation in the history of the race, something that can be compared with habit, which is indeed second nature though not a new quality but only a quantitative progression, is due to anxiety having now entered the world in another sense. Sin entered into anxiety, but sin once more brought with it anxiety. The fact is that the actuality of sin is an actuality with no subsistence. Sin's continuity is, on the one hand, the possibility that causes anxiety. On the other hand, the possibility of a salvation is once again a nothing which the individual both loves and fears, for this is always possibility's relation to individuality. Only in that instant when salvation is actually posited is this anxiety overcome. Man's and creation's eager longing* is not, as has been sentimentally thought, a sweet longing; for it to be that, sin would have to be disarmed. Someone who wants truly to familiarize himself with the state of sin, and with what the expectation of salvation might be like, will doubtless recognize this and be a little ashamed of

* [Romans 8:19]

an aesthetic absence of shame. In the human being, as long as the question is only one of expectation, the power is still in the hands of sin, and sin of course conceives the expectation in a hostile manner. (This will be dealt with later.)[1] When salvation is posited, anxiety is left behind along with possibility. This does not mean that it is annihilated but that, if rightly used, it plays another role (see Chapter V).

The anxiety that sin brings in with it is really only present when the individual itself posits sin, and yet this anxiety is obscurely present as a more or a less in the quantitative history of the race. So even here one will come across the phenomenon that a person seems to become guilty simply through anxiety about himself, something of which there could be no question in Adam's case. It is nevertheless true that every individual becomes guilty only through himself, but here the quantitative aspect in relation to the race has reached its maximum and will have it in its power to confuse every view unless one insists on the distinction specified earlier between the quantitative accumulation and the qualitative leap. This phenomenon will be considered later.[2] Generally it is ignored, which is of course easiest. Or it is construed sentimentally and touchingly, with a cowardly sympathy which thanks God for not having become like that,* yet without understanding that a thanksgiving of that kind is treason against both God and oneself, and without reflecting that life always has analogous phenomena in store that one perhaps will not escape. Sympathy one must indeed have, but sympathy is true only when it is admitted, deep down, that what has happened to one person can happen to all. Only then does one benefit both oneself and others. The physician at an insane asylum who is foolish enough to believe that

* [Cf. Luke 18:10–14]

he is eternally wise, and that his bit of reason is insured against all harm in this life, is in one way wiser than the demented, but he is also more foolish, nor is he likely to heal many.

Anxiety, then, means two things: the anxiety in which the individual posits sin through the qualitative leap, and the anxiety that comes in and enters with sin, and in that respect also enters quantitatively into the world every time an individual posits sin.

——————

It is not my intention to write a learned work or waste time looking for corroboration in literature. Often the literary examples adduced in psychologies lack real psychological authority. They stand as an isolated fact attested *notarialiter* [by notary public], but just for that reason one doesn't know whether to laugh or weep at such attempts by a lonely starched collar to form some kind of a rule. Someone who has occupied himself with psychology and with psychological observation according to some standard will have acquired a general human flexibility that enables him straightaway to construct his example which, even if it lacks factual authority, has authority of another kind. Just as the psychological observer should be more nimble than a tightrope dancer, so as to be able to unbend to others and imitate their attitudes, and just as his silence in the moment of confidence should be seductive and sensual, so that what is secret can have the pleasure of slipping out to mumble to itself in this artificially contrived obscurity and silence, so too should he possess a poetic primitiveness in his soul so as to be able straightaway to create what is whole and regular out of what in the individual is present always only partially and irregularly. Once he has perfected these, he will have no need to fetch his examples from literary anthologies and to serve up half-dead reminiscences, but will bring his observations altogether fresh from the water, wriggling and sparkling in their iridescence. Nor will he need to rush himself off his feet to become alive to something. On the contrary, he should sit quite still in his own room, like a plain clothes detective who nevertheless knows all that is going on.[3] What he needs he can fashion straightaway. What he needs is immediately at hand by virtue of his general practice, just as in a well-equipped house one has no need to carry water from the street but thanks to high pressure has it on one's level. He is so well oriented in human life, and his eyes are so inquisitorially sharp that should he begin to doubt, he knows where to look for and easily come upon an individuality that can serve passably for his own mental experimentation. His observation should be as reliable as anyone's, even if unsupported by references to names and erudite quotations, such as that there once lived in Saxony a peasant girl in whom a physician observed . . . , that in Rome there was once an emperor of whom a historian relates that . . . , etc., as if such things happen only once in a thousand years. What interest can psychology have in that? No, it is everything, what happens every day if only the observer is present. If he takes the precaution of controlling his observation, his observation will have the stamp of freshness and possess the interest of the actual. To do so he apes every mood in himself, every psychic state that he discovers in another. He then sees whether he can delude the other by the imitation, whether he can draw him along into the further performance, which is his own creation based on the implication of his thought [i *Kraft af Ideen*—lit. on the strength of the idea]. If one wants to observe a passion in this way, one chooses one's individual. What counts now is to be still, silent, and inconspicuous so as to discover the individual's secret.

One must then practice what one has learned until able to delude the individual. Then one composes the passion and appears before the individual in the passion's preternatural size. If this is done correctly, the individual will feel an indescribable relief and satisfaction, just as an insane person when someone has found and poetically grasped his fixation and then proceeds to take it further. If it does not succeed, the reason may be a defect in the operation, but it can also be because the individual was a poor example.

§1

Objective Anxiety

O ur use of the expression "objective anxiety" might almost lead one to think of the anxiety that belongs to innocence, the anxiety that is freedom's reflection within itself in its possibility. It would be an inadequate rejoinder to this to object that it overlooks the fact that we now find ourselves at another juncture in the investigation. We are better served by being reminded, on the contrary, that objective anxiety's distinctness lies in its separation from subjective anxiety, a distinction that could not be made in Adam's state of innocence. Subjective anxiety is, in the strictest sense, that anxiety which is posited in the individual and is the outcome of its sin. Anxiety in that sense will be discussed in a later chapter.[4] But if the term is taken in that sense, the contrast provided by objective anxiety no longer applies and anxiety appears exactly as what it is, namely the subjective. The distinction between objective and subjective anxiety belongs, therefore, to a consideration of the world and the state of innocence in the later individual. The division comes to light here insofar as subjective anxiety now signifies the anxiety present in the individual's state of innocence, which corresponds to that of Adam but differs from Adam's quantitatively due to the quantifying effect of the generation. By objective anxiety we understand, on the other hand, the reflection of that generational sinfulness in the entire world.

In §2 of the previous chapter we were reminded that the expression "through Adam's sin, sinfulness *entered the world*" contained an outward reflection. Here is the place to return to that expression in order to recover it in its true meaning. The instant Adam has posited sin, consideration turns from him to the beginning of every later individual's sin, for now the generation is posited. To posit the sinfulness of the human race through Adam's sin as though in the same sense as his walking erect, etc., is to cancel the concept of the individual. This was explained earlier, where objection was also made to the experimenting inquisitiveness that would treat sin as a curiosity, and the dilemma also raised that it would be necessary to envisage either a questioner who had no idea even of what he was asking about or a questioner who knew and whose pretended ignorance became a new sin.

If all this is now adhered to, that expression will possess its limited truth. The first posits the quality and Adam then posits sin in himself but also for the human race. However, the concept of race is too abstract for the positing of so concrete a category as sin, which is posited precisely through the single individual positing it himself as the single individual. Sinfulness in the race then becomes only a quantitative approximating, though one that has its beginning with Adam. This is where Adam's greater importance lies, above that of every other individual in the race, and this is where the truth of that expression lies. Even an ortho-doxy willing to understand itself has to admit this, seeing that it teaches that nature as well as the human race fell through Adam's sin, even if in regard to nature it will hardly do to have sin enter as the *quality* of sin.

Sin's entering the world had significance for the whole of cre-ation. The effect of this sin on the nonhuman aspect of life [*Til-værelse*] I have called objective anxiety.

What this means can be indicated by calling attention to the scriptural expression ἀποκαραδοκία τῆς κτίσεως [the eager long-ing of creation] (Rom. 8:19). Insofar as there can be talk of an eager longing, it goes without saying that creation is in a state of imperfection. One often fails to see with expressions and defini-tions such as longing, eager longing, expectation, etc., that these involve an antecedent state, and that this state is therefore present and simultaneously makes itself felt as that in which the longing unfolds. This state of expectancy is not one that the person has fallen into by accident, etc., thus finding himself a total stranger in it; he is producing it himself at the same time. The expression for such a longing is anxiety; for it is in anxiety that the state out of which he longs to be proclaims itself, and proclaims itself because the longing alone is not enough to save him.

In what sense creation sank into depravity through Adam's sin, how freedom in being posited with the positing of its own misuse thus cast a reflection of possibility and a *frisson* of com-plicity over creation, in what sense this had to happen because the human being is the synthesis whose most extreme opposites were posited, and whose one opposite became precisely through the human being's sin a still far more extreme opposite than it was before—all this has no place in a psychological deliberation but belongs to dogmatics, to the Atonement, in the explanation of which this science explains sinfulness's presupposition.*

This anxiety in creation can indeed properly be called objective anxiety. It is not brought forth by creation but by the fact that Adam's sin placed it in an entirely different light, and insofar as sin continues to enter the world, sensuousness is constantly degraded to mean sinfulness. One can readily see that this interpretation also keeps an eye on itself in the sense that it wards off the rationalistic view according to which sensuousness as such is sinfulness.[5] After sin has entered the world, and every time sin enters the world, sensuousness becomes sinfulness. But what it becomes is not what it was previously. Franz Baader[6] has protested often enough against the proposition that finitude and sensuousness as such are sinfulness. But unless care is taken here, one gets Pelagianism[7] from quite another side. In his definition, Baader took no account of the history of the race. In the human race, quantitatively (i.e., nonessentially) sensuousness is sinfulness, but in relation to the individual not so, until by positing sin the individual again makes sensuousness sinfulness.

Some men of Schelling's† school have paid special attention

---

* Here is how to deploy dogmatics. Each science must have above all a robust sense of its beginning and not live in promiscuity with others. If dogmatics begins by wanting to explain sinfulness, or by wanting to explain sin's actuality, nothing "dogmatic" will ever come out of it, and the whole existence of dogmatics will become problematic and diffuse.

† In Schelling himself there is often talk of anxiety, wrath, anguish, suffering, etc. But talk of this kind should always be treated with a little suspicion so as not to mistake what follows sin in the creation for what Schelling also characterizes as states and moods in God. What he designates by these expressions are, if I may say so, the deity's creative birth pangs. Such figurative expressions are in part what he himself called the negative and in Hegel became the negative more closely

to the alteration* that creation has incurred through sin. There
has also been talk of the anxiety that is supposed to occur in
inanimate nature. The effect is however weakened when at one
moment we are led to believe that what we have is a nature philosophy cleverly handled with help from dogmatics, and at the

---

defined as the dialectical (το ἕτερον). The ambiguity is evident also in
Schelling because he speaks of a melancholy spread over nature as well
as of a heaviness of spirit in the deity. But above all, Schelling's main
thought is that anxiety and the rest characterize in particular the suffer-
ings of the deity in coming to create. In Berlin he expressed the same
more definitely by comparing God with [Johann Wolfgang von] Goethe
[(1749–1832), the German poet, dramatist, statesman, and natural sci-
entist] and Johannes von Müller [(1752–1809), a Swiss historian and
political journalist], both of whom felt well only when producing, and
also by calling attention to the fact that a bliss of this kind that cannot
declare itself is unhappiness. I mention this here because his remark has
already appeared in print in a pamphlet by [Philipp Konrad] Marheineke
[(1780–1846), a Protestant theologian whose lectures Kierkegaard had
attended when in Berlin in 1841–42]. Marheineke wants to ironize it.
This one ought not to do, for a vigorous and full-blooded anthropomor-
phism has considerable merit. The mistake is however a different one,
and here we can see an example of how strange everything becomes
when metaphysics and dogmatics are corrupted by treating dogmatics
metaphysically and metaphysics dogmatically.

*The word *alteration* in Danish expresses the ambiguity very nicely.
Alterere is used in the sense of changing, distorting, bringing out of its
original state (the thing becomes another), but one also speaks of
becoming *altereret* in the sense of becoming frightened, just because
this is basically the unfailing first accompaniment. As far as I know, the
Latin scholar doesn't use the word at all but oddly enough uses *adulter-
are* [to commit adultery, to adulterate or debase]. The Frenchman says
altérer les monnaie [to counterfeit the money] and *être altéré* [to be
frightened]. With us, the word is used in everyday speech only in the
sense of being frightened, and thus one hears the ordinary person say,
"Jeg ble ganske altereret [I was quite scared]." I have at any rate heard a
basket woman say it.

next moment a dogmatic definition bathing in the glow of a magical wonder from contemplation of nature.

Here, though, I break off what I have adduced just to carry us for a moment beyond the bounds of the present investigation. Anxiety, as it appeared in Adam, will never return, since it was through him that sinfulness entered the world. For that reason there are now two analogues to Adam's anxiety: the objective anxiety in nature and the subjective anxiety in the individual, of which the latter contains a more and the first a less than the anxiety in Adam.

§2

Subjective Anxiety

The more reflected one dares to posit the anxiety, the easier it may seem for anxiety to switch over into guilt. But here it is important not to let oneself be taken in by terms of approximation: a "more" cannot produce the leap, and in truth no "easier" can make it more easy to explain. If a grip is not kept on this, there is a risk of suddenly coming upon a phenomenon where everything goes so easily that the transition becomes a simple transition, or else the risk of never daring to bring one's thought to a conclusion because purely empirical observation can never come to an end. Therefore, even if anxiety becomes more and more reflected, the guilt which emerges in anxiety through the qualitative leap retains the same accountability as that of Adam, and the anxiety the same ambiguity.

Wanting to deny that every later individual has, and must be assumed to have had, a state of innocence analogous to Adam's would shock everyone as much as it would nullify all thought, because then there would be an individual who was not an individual but related to its species merely as a specimen, even if, identified as an individual, that individual would at the same time be considered guilty.

Anxiety can be compared with dizziness. He whose eye happens to look down into the yawning abyss becomes dizzy. But what is the reason? It is just as much his own eye as the abyss, for suppose he had not looked down. It is in this way that anxiety is the dizziness of freedom that emerges when spirit wants to posit the synthesis, and freedom now looks down into its own possibility and then grabs hold of finiteness to support itself. In this dizziness freedom subsides. Further, psychology cannot and will not go. In that very instant everything is changed, and in raising itself up again freedom sees that it is guilty. Between these two moments lies the leap, which no science has explained and which no science can explain. The person who becomes guilty in anxiety becomes as ambiguously guilty as it is possible to become. Anxiety is a feminine effeteness in which freedom swoons. Psychologically speaking, the fall into sin always occurs in a state of enervation. But anxiety is also the most selfish of things, and no concrete expression of freedom is as selfish as the possibility of every concretion. This is again the overwhelming factor that determines the individual's ambiguous relation, sympathetic and antipathetic. In anxiety there is the selfish infinity of possibility, which does not tempt like a choice but disquietens seductively with its sweet apprehensiveness.

In the later individual, anxiety is more reflective. This can be put by saying that the nothing that is the object of anxiety becomes as though more and more a something. We don't say that it actually becomes a something, or actually means something; we don't say that, instead of a nothing, sin or something else should now be substituted, since what goes here for the later individual's innocence also goes for Adam's. All of this is only for freedom and only when the single individual itself posits sin through the qualitative leap. Here the nothing of anxiety is a complex of presentiments that reflect themselves in themselves, becoming closer and closer to the individual, notwithstanding that essentially, in anxiety, they signify nothing, not indeed, be it noted, a nothing that the individual has nothing to do with, but a nothing in lively communication with the ignorance of innocence. This reflexivity is a predisposition which, before the individual becomes guilty, still essentially signifies nothing, whereas when, through the qualitative leap, the individual became guilty, it is the presupposition in which the individual goes beyond itself because sin presupposes itself, not of course before being posited (that would be predestination), but presupposes itself in being posited.

We shall now consider in a little more detail that something which the nothing of anxiety can signify in the later individual. In the psychological deliberation it truly counts for something. But the psychological deliberation does not forget that if an individual were to become guilty as a matter of course through this something, then all consideration would be brought to nothing.

This something which signifies hereditary sin *stricte sic dicta* [in the strict sense of the word] is:

A. The Result of the Relation of Generation

It is obvious that we are not discussing anything that can occupy physicians, whether one is born deformed, and so on; nor is there any question of arriving at results by way of statistical surveys. Here, as everywhere, it is important that the mood be the right

one. When a person has been taught that hailstones and crop fail-
ures may be attributed to the devil, this can be very well meant,
but essentially it is a farfetched notion that weakens the concept
of evil and introduces an almost jesting note into it, just as it is an
aesthetical pleasantry to speak of a stupid devil. So when the historical aspect is given so one-sided a significance in dealing with
the concept of "faith" that its primitive originality in the individual
is overlooked, faith becomes in the end a finite pettiness instead
of a free infinitude. The result is that faith can come to be spoken
of in the manner of Hieronymus in Holberg,[8] who says of Erasmus Montanus that his views on faith are heretical because he
thinks the earth is round and not flat, as one local generation after
another had believed. In that way, one might become a heretic in
one's faith by wearing wide breeches when all the locals wear tight
trousers. To offer statistical surveys of the incidence of sinfulness,
to draw a map of it where the color and relief help the eye to take
it all in at once, is to try to treat sin as a curiosity of nature, not
to be removed but to be reckoned just like atmospheric pressure
and rainfall. The resulting mean, or arithmetical average, is quite
otherwise nonsensical than in those purely empirical sciences. It
would be a very ridiculous abracadabra should anyone seriously
suggest that sinfulness averages $3\frac{3}{8}$ inches in every person, or that
in Languedoc the average is only $2\frac{1}{4}$ inches, while in Bretagne it is
$3\frac{7}{8}$. The examples here are no more superfluous than those in the
Introduction, drawn as they are from the compass of the sphere
within which what follows is to turn.

Through sin, sensuousness became sinfulness. This proposition has a double meaning: through sin sensuousness becomes
sinfulness, and through Adam sin came into the world. These
two terms must constantly hold their own against each other,

since otherwise what is asserted will be something untrue. That at one time sensuousness became sinfulness is the history of the generation, but that sensuousness becomes sinfulness, that is the qualitative leap of the individual.

We were reminded (Chapter I, §6) that the creation of Eve already metaphorically prefigures the outcome of the relation of generation. In a sense, she signifies that which is derived. Something derived is never as perfect as the original.* Here, however, the difference is merely quantitative. Essentially the later individual is just as original as the first. The difference *in pleno* [common] to all later individuals is derivation, but for the single individual derivation may again signify a more or a less.

This derivation of the woman also contains the explanation of the sense in which she is weaker than the man, something that has been assumed in all ages, whether it is a pasha speaking or a romantic knight. The difference is not, however, otherwise than that the man and the woman are essentially alike despite the dissimilarity. The expression of the difference is that anxiety is more reflected in Eve than in Adam. This is because the woman is more sensuous than the man. Here of course it is not a matter of an empirical state, or of an average number, but of the dissimilarity in the synthesis. If in one part of the synthesis there is a "more," a result will be that when spirit posits itself, the cleft becomes deeper and in freedom's possibility anxiety will find greater scope. In the Genesis account it is Eve who seduces Adam. But it by no means follows that her guilt is greater than Adam's, and still less

---

*This, of course, applies only to the human race, because the individual is qualified as spirit. In animal species every subsequent specimen is, on the contrary, just as good as the first, or, more correctly, being the first here means absolutely nothing.

that anxiety is an imperfection, seeing that, on the contrary, its magnitude is a prophecy of that of the perfection.

Already here the investigation has seen that the proportion of sensuousness corresponds to that of anxiety. Once the relation of generation appears, whatever was said of Eve becomes simply an intimation of every later individual's relation to Adam, namely, that just as sensuousness has been increased in the generation, so too has there been an increase in anxiety. So the result of the relation of generation signifies a "more" such that no individual can escape it, it being a "more" to all later individuals in their relation to Adam, but never such that the individual comes essentially to differ from Adam.

However, before passing on to this, I shall first shed a little more light on the proposition that the woman is more sensuous than the man and has more anxiety.

That the woman is more sensuous than the man is immediately apparent in her physical organism. To deal more particularly with this is not my concern but a task for physiology. However, I shall present my proposition in a different way, introducing her aesthetically under her ideal aspect, which is beauty, and bringing to mind that the very fact that this is her ideal aspect itself indicates that she is more sensuous than the man. I shall then introduce her ethically under her ideal aspect, which is procreation, bringing to mind that the circumstance that this is indeed her ideal aspect indicates precisely that she is more sensuous than the man.

When beauty has to reign, it brings about a synthesis from which spirit is excluded. This is the secret of all Greek culture. There is in a sense a repose, a tranquil solemnity about Greek beauty, but for this very reason there is also an anxiety which the Greek doubtless did not notice even though his plastic beauty trembled with it. The reason for absence of concern in Greek beauty is that spirit is excluded, but for the same reason there is also a profound and unexplained sorrow. Thus sensuousness is not sinfulness but an unexplained riddle that causes unrest. This naïveté is accompanied therefore by an inexplicable nothing, which is that of anxiety.

It is true that Greek beauty conceives of the man and of the woman as similarly not spiritual, but within that likeness it makes a distinction nevertheless. The spiritual has its expression in the face. In manly beauty the face and its expression are more essential than in womanly beauty, although the eternal youthfulness of plastic art constantly prevents the deeper spirituality from emerging. To further expand on this is not my task, but I shall point to the dissimilarity with a single suggestion. Venus is essentially just as beautiful when represented as sleeping, yes, possibly at her most beautiful, yet sleeping is exactly the state that expresses the absence of spirit. For this reason, the older and the more spiritually developed the individuality, the less beautiful it is in sleep, whereas the child is most beautiful in sleep. Venus emerges from the sea, and is represented in an attitude of repose, or in an attitude that precisely reduces the expression of the face to what is inessential. In representing an Apollo, however, it would be no more appropriate to have him sleep than it would to have a Jupiter do so. Apollo would become ugly and Jupiter ridiculous. An exception might be made of Bacchus, but in Greek art he represents an indifference between manly and womanly beauty, as a result of which his forms are also feminine. With a Ganymede, however, the expression of the face is already more essential.[9]

When beauty became something else, romanticism nevertheless repeats the dissimilarity within the essential likeness. While the history of spirit (and just this is the secret of spirit, that it has a history) dares to impress itself on the man's countenance in a way that forgets everything if only the imprint is distinct and noble, the woman will make her effect as a totality in another way, even though the face has acquired a greater significance than in classical art. The expression must be that of a totality that has no history. Therefore silence is not only the woman's greatest wisdom but also her highest beauty.

Viewed ethically, woman culminates in procreation. There-fore the Scriptures say that her desire shall be for her husband.[*] Although it is also true that the husband's desire is for her, his life does not culminate in this desire, unless his life is worthless or lost. But the fact that woman culminates in this shows precisely that she is more sensuous.

The woman is more anxious than the man. This is not because she has less physical strength, etc., for that kind of anxiety is not at all at issue here; it is because she is more sensuous than the man and yet, like him, has essentially the character of spirit. What has often been said about her, that she is the weaker sex, is for me a matter of great indifference, because she could for that reason very well be less anxious than the man. Anxiety is constantly to be conceived here in terms of freedom. So when, in the teeth of all analogy, the Genesis story represents the woman as seducing the man, this on further reflection is quite correct; for that seduction is precisely a feminine seduction, since it was only through Eve that Adam could be seduced by the serpent.[†] Other-

[*] [Genesis 3:16]
[†] [Genesis 3:6, 12]

wise in matters of seduction, linguistic usage (charm, cajole, etc.) always stresses the man's superiority.

I shall simply indicate through an imaginary situation what all experience may be assumed to acknowledge. If I imagine an innocent young girl and let a man fasten a covetous gaze upon her, she becomes anxious. She may also become indignant, etc., but first she becomes anxious. If, on the other hand, I picture a young woman fastening her covetous gaze upon an innocent young man, his mood will not be anxiety but a shamefacedness at most, mingled with disgust, precisely because he is characterized more as spirit.

Through Adam's sin there came sinfulness into the world, and sexuality, and for him this came to signify sinfulness. The sexual was posited. There has been a great deal of chatter in the world, both spoken and written, about naïveté. Only innocence, meanwhile, is naïve. But it is also ignorant. Once the sexual is brought to consciousness, it is thoughtlessness, affectation, to speak of naïveté, and at times what is worse, a disguise for lust. But from the fact that a man is no longer naïve it by no means follows that he sins. It is only these vapid flatteries that lead people on, precisely by diverting attention from the true, from the moral.

Up until now the whole question of the significance of the sexual, and its significance in the particular spheres, has been given unquestionably poor answers and has above all very rarely been answered in the right mood. Offering witticisms about the sexual is a cheap art, admonishing is not difficult, and preaching about it in a way that avoids the difficulty is not hard; but to speak of it in a truly human way is an art. Leaving it to the stage and the pulpit to undertake the answer in a way that each is embarrassed by what the other says, so that the one explanation differs glaringly from the other, is really to abandon it all and lay upon people themselves the heavy burden—one for which they are unwilling to lift a finger*—of finding meaning in both explanations while the respective teachers continue lecturing on just the one or the other. The incongruity of this situation would have long since been recognized if in our day people had not perfected themselves in the thoughtless waste of a life so beautifully planned, and in thoughtlessly joining in noisily whenever there is talk about one or another grand, huge idea, in the fulfillment of which they unite in an unshakable faith in the power of association, even if it is a faith just as marvelous as that of the alehouse keeper who sold his beer for a penny under cost price and still counted on a profit, "since it is the *numbers* that does it." Seeing this is how things are, it doesn't surprise me that no one pays attention these days to such a deliberation. But this I do know: had Socrates lived now, he would have thought on such things and would have done it better or, if I may say so, more divinely than I can, and I am convinced that he would have said to me: "Ah! my dear fellow, in considering such things, which are well worth pondering, you do rightly; yes! one could sit and talk through whole nights and yet never finish sounding out the wonders of human nature." And to me this assurance is worth infinitely more than the Bravo! of all my contemporaries. For this assurance makes my soul unshakable, while the applause would cause it to doubt.

The sexual as such is not the sinful. Genuine ignorance about it, when essentially present, is reserved for the beast alone, which is therefore a slave of blind instinct and moves in the dark. An ignorance, but which is also an ignorance of what is not, is that of

* [Matthew 23:4]

the child. Innocence is a knowledge that signifies ignorance. Its distinctness from moral ignorance is easily shown by the fact that the latter is to be defined in terms of a knowing. With innocence there begins a knowing that has ignorance as its first attribute. This is the concept of modesty (*Schaam*).[10] There is an anxiety in modesty because spirit is defined at the extremity of the difference of the synthesis in a way that identifies spirit not merely as body but as body with the sexual difference. Modesty is indeed a knowing of that difference nonetheless, though not as a relation to that difference, which is to say, the drive as such is not present. The real significance of modesty is that spirit cannot, so to speak, own up to the extremity of the synthesis. That is why the anxiety found in modesty is enormously ambiguous. There is no trace of sensuous desire and yet there is a sense of shame. Shame of what? Of nothing. And yet the individual may die of shame, and wounded modesty is the deepest pain because it is the most inexplicable of all. That is why the anxiety in modesty can awaken by itself. Yet what is the case here, naturally, is that it is not desire that plays this part. An example of the latter is found in one of Friedrich Schlegel's tales (*Sämmtliche Werke*, vol. 7, p. 15, the story of Merlin).[11]

In modesty, sexual difference is posited but not in relation to its other. That occurs in the drive. But since the drive is not instinct, or simply instinct, it *eo ipso* [by virtue of that very fact] has a $\tau\epsilon\lambda o\varsigma$ [end or aim], which is propagation, while the pending state is love, pure eroticism. All the time spirit is still not posited. Once it is posited, not merely as constituting the synthesis but as spirit, the erotic is over. The highest pagan expression for this is that the erotic is the comical. This must not, of course, be understood in the way that a sensualist might think of the erotic as comic and material for his lascivious wit; it is the power of intel-

ligence and its preponderance that neutralize both the erotic and
the moral relation to the erotic in the indifference of spirit. This
has a very profound basis. The anxiety in modesty arose from
spirit feeling alien; now that spirit has triumphed completely, it
sees the sexual as alien and as the comic. This freedom of the
spirit was something that modesty naturally could not possess.
The sexual is the expression of the huge contradiction (*Wider-
spruch*) that the immortal spirit is defined as *genus* [gender]. This
contradiction expresses itself in the deep *Schaam* that conceals
this contradiction and dares not understand it. Within the erotic,
the contradiction is understood in terms of beauty, for beauty is
precisely the unity of the psychic and the somatic. But this contradiction, which the erotic transfigures in beauty, is for spirit at
once both the beautiful and the comic. Spirit's expression for the
erotic is therefore that it is simultaneously the beautiful and the
comic. Here there is no sensuous association in the direction of
the erotic, for that is sensuality, in which case the individual lies
far beneath the beauty of the erotic. Rather, it is the maturity
of spirit. This, naturally, is something that in its purity very few
people have understood. Socrates did so however. So when Xenophon[12] has him saying that one should love ugly women, here, as
with all else that Xenophon lends his hand to, he makes a repellent, narrow-minded philistinism out of those words, which is
least of all like Socrates. The meaning is this, that he has reduced
the erotic to indifference, and he expresses the contradiction that
underlies the comic correctly in the corresponding ironic contradiction that one should love those who are ugly.* But such a

---

*This is how we must understand what Socrates said to Critobulus [a
student of Socrates's] about the kiss. I think it must be obvious to everyone that it would have been impossible for Socrates in all seriousness to

view very rarely occurs in its lofty purity. It requires an unusual interplay between a fortunate historical development and primitive talent. If any such objection is remotely possible, the view is repellent and an affectation.

In Christianity, the religious has suspended the erotic, not merely through an ethical misunderstanding as the sinful, but as

---

have spoken with such pathos about the danger of the kiss, and also that he was no anxious ninny who dared not look at a woman. No doubt in southern countries and among more passionate peoples the kiss means more than here in the north (on this one may look up [Erykias] Puteanus [(1574–1646), a Dutch historian] in a letter to John Bapt. Saccum [a secretary in the Milan council]: *nesciunt nostrae virgines ullum libidinis rudimentum osculis aut osculis inesse, ideoque fruuntur. Vestrae sciunt* [our (Belgian) maidens do not know that a kiss or a glance of the eye can be the beginning of lust, and therefore abandon themselves to it. Your Italian maidens know it]. Cf. [Martin von] Kempius [Kempen (1642–1683)], *Dissertatio de osculis*, in Bayle). Still, it is unlike Socrates both as an ironist and as a moralist to speak in this way. To come on too heavily as moralist is to awaken desire and tempt the pupil almost against his will to become ironical toward the teacher. Socrates's relation to Aspasia points the same way. He associated with her quite unconcerned about the ambiguous life she led. He wanted only to learn from her (Athenaeus [Naucratita (c. 200 BC), a grammarian]), and she seems to have had talent in that way, since it is told that husbands brought their wives along to Aspasia to learn from her. But then Socrates, as soon as Aspasia wanted to impress him with her loveliness, has presumably explained to her that one ought to love ugly women, and that she should not exert her charms any further since, for his own purposes, he had enough in Xantippe (cf. Xenophon's account of Socrates's view of his relation to Xantippe [Socrates's reputedly shrewish wife]). Regrettably, since people repeatedly approach their reading of everything with preconceived opinions, it is no wonder that everyone has a fixed notion that a Cynic is more or less a profligate. Yet here too it might be possible, exactly among the Cynics [forerunners of the Hippies, who rejected regulation and sought to live naturally], to find an example of that view of the erotic as the comic.

the indifferent, because in spirit there is no difference between man and woman.* Here the erotic is not neutralized through irony but suspended, because Christianity's tendency is to bring the spirit further. When, in modesty, spirit becomes anxious and shy about arraying itself in the differentiation of sex, the individuality suddenly leaps off and instead of pervading the gender difference ethically, grabs hold of an explanation from spirit's highest sphere. This is one side of the monastic view, whether further defined as ethical rigorism or as predominantly contemplation.†

Just as anxiety is posited in modesty, so is it present in all erotic enjoyment, and not because it is sinful, not at all, which is why neither is it of any help if the minister blesses the couple ten times. Even when the erotic expresses itself as beautifully, purely, and morally as possible, undisturbed in its joy by any lascivious reflection, anxiety is still present, not, however, as a disturbing but as an accompanying factor.

Undertaking observations in this matter is extremely difficult. The observer must in particular exercise the caution taken by physicians who never take the pulse without making sure that it is not their own pulse they feel but that of the patient. Similarly, one must take care that the movement one discovers is not one's own restlessness in carrying out the observation. It is quite certain, however, that in describing love, in however pure and innocent a light they present it, all poets posit anxiety along with it. Going

---

* [1 Corinthians 12:13; Galatians 3:28]

† However strange it may seem to someone unused to facing the phenomena boldly, there is nevertheless a perfect analogy between Socrates's ironic view of the erotic as comical and a monk's relation to *mulieres subintroductae* [women brought in secretly]. The abuse naturally concerns only those who have a liking for abuse.

further into this is a matter for the aesthetician. But why this anxiety? It is because spirit cannot take part in the culmination of the
erotic. I will speak in the manner of the Greeks. Spirit is indeed
present, because it is spirit that establishes the synthesis, but it
cannot express itself in the erotic; it feels alien. It is as though it
said to the erotic: "My dear! Here I cannot be a third party, so I
shall go into hiding for the time being." But just this is anxiety,
and modesty as well. For it is a great foolishness to assume that
the church's marriage ceremony or the husband's faithfulness in
keeping to his wife alone is all that is needed.* Many a marriage
has been profaned even if it was not through a stranger. But when
the erotic is pure, innocent, and beautiful, then this anxiety is
friendly and mild, and the poets are therefore right when they
speak of a sweet anxiousness. It goes without saying, however,
that anxiety is greater in the woman than in the man.

Let us now return to our earlier topic, namely the result of the
relation of generation in the individual, which is the "more" that
every later individual has with regard to Adam. In the moment
of conception, spirit is furthest away and for that reason the
anxiety at its greatest. In this anxiety, the new individual comes
into being. In the moment of birth, anxiety culminates a second
time in the woman, and that instant the new individual enters
the world. That giving birth is anxiety is well known. Physiology
has its explanation, and psychology must have its explanation too.
In childbirth the woman is again at the edge of one extreme of
the synthesis, and spirit therefore trembles, for in that moment it
does not have its task, it is as if suspended. Anxiety, however, is
an expression of the perfection of human nature; it is therefore

* [Cf. Genesis 2:24]

only among lower peoples that one finds the analogue of the easy delivery of animals.

But the more anxiety, the more sensuousness. The procreated individual is more sensuous than the original, and this "more" is the common "more" of the generation for every later individual with regard to Adam.

But this "more" of anxiety and sensuousness for every later individual in relation to Adam may of course signify a more and less in the particular individual. Here lie differences that are in truth so terrible that surely no one dares to ponder them in a deeper sense, that is, with genuine human sympathy, unless convinced with an unshakable firmness that never in the world has there been, or ever will be, a "more" such that by a simple transition it transforms the quantitative into the qualitative. What Scripture teaches, that God punishes the children for the iniquity of their fathers to the third and fourth generations,* life proclaims loudly enough. Wanting to talk oneself out of this dreadful fact by explaining the saying as a Jewish teaching does not help. Christianity has never consented to privileging each individual to make a fresh start in an outward way. Each individual begins in a historical nexus and nature's consequences are still as valid as ever. Except for this, that Christianity teaches each individual to lift itself above that "more," and it condemns the individual who does not do that for not being willing to do so.

Just because sensuousness here is defined as a "more," spirit's anxiety in assuming responsibility for it becomes a greater anxiety. The maximum here is the dreadful fact that *anxiety about sin produces sin*. If we let evil desire, concupiscence, etc., be innate in the

---

* |Exodus 20:5]

individual, we lose the ambiguity in which the individual becomes both guilty and innocent. In the faintness of anxiety, the individual swoons and is for that very reason both guilty and innocent.

I shall not cite detailed examples here of this infinitely fluctuating more and less. To have any significance they would need to be given an extensive and painstaking aesthetic-psychological treatment.

B. The Outcome of the Historical Relation

If I were to express here in one clause the "more" that every later individual has in relation to Adam, I would say it is: that sensuousness can signify sinfulness, that is, this obscure knowledge of it, along with an obscure knowledge of whatever else sin can signify along with a misunderstood appropriation of the historical *de te fabula narratur* [the story is told about you], in which the point, the individual primitivity, is excluded, and the individual without further ado mistakes itself for the human race and its history. We say not that sensuousness is sinfulness, but that sin makes it sinfulness. If we now consider the later individual, then every such individual has a historical environment in which it can become apparent that sensuousness can signify sinfulness. For the individual itself, sensuousness does not signify this, but this knowing gives anxiety a "more." So spirit is posited in relation to the opposite not only of sensuousness, but also of sinfulness. Of course, as yet the innocent individual does not understand this knowing, for it can only be understood qualitatively, but this knowing is again a new possibility, such that freedom as it relates in its possibility to the sensuous becomes still more anxiety.

That this common "more" can indicate a more and a less for

the particular individual goes without saying. Attention is thus drawn to a grand differentia. After Christianity had come into the world and redemption was posited, sensuousness was cast in an oppositional light that was not to be found in paganism, and which of all things serves to confirm the proposition that sensuousness is sinfulness.

Within the Christian differentia, this "more" may again signify a more and a less. This lies in the particular innocent individual's relation to its historical environment. The most dissimilar things may produce the same effect in this respect. Freedom's possibility announces itself in anxiety. A reminder may now be enough to bring an individual to collapse in anxiety (remember that I speak as always only psychologically and never nullify the qualitative leap), and this despite the reminder naturally being intended to do just the opposite. Sight of the sinful may save one individual and ruin another. A joke may have the same effect as seriousness and vice versa. Speech and silence can both produce an effect that is the opposite of that intended. There are no limits in this respect. So here again one observes the correctness of the attribution that this is a quantitative more or less, for after all, the quantitative is precisely the infinite limit.

I shall not pursue this with any further experiential projections here, since that would detain us. But life is rich enough if one only knows how to see. There is no need to travel to Paris and London—and it does not help if one cannot see.

As for that, anxiety has the same ambiguity here as it has always. At this point a maximum may appear corresponding to the one just mentioned, that the individual in anxiety about sin produces sin, in this case: *the individual, in anxiety not about becoming guilty but about being seen as guilty, becomes guilty.*

The ultimate "more" in this respect, furthermore, is that from its earliest awakening an individual is placed and influenced in such a way that sensuousness has become identical with sinfulness, and this ultimate "more" will appear in the most painful form of a collision if in the whole surrounding world absolutely no support is found. If to this ultimate "more" is added the confusion that the individual mistakes itself for its historical knowledge of sinfulness, and in the pallor of anxiety straightaway places itself *qua* individual under the same category, forgetting freedom's "If you do likewise"—then we have that ultimate "more."

What has been briefly suggested here, that it takes a fairly rich experience to grasp how much has been said, and said definitely and clearly, is something that has been discussed often enough. The discussion is commonly called: "On the power of the example." Unquestionably, much has been well said on this matter, if not exactly in these recent superphilosophical times. But what is often missing is a psychological middle term, namely, the explanation of what it takes for the example to have such power. Moreover, the subject is sometimes treated in these circles a little too carelessly, and without noticing that a single little mistake in the smallest detail can throw the huge balance sheet of life into confusion. Psychological attention is fixed exclusively upon the particular phenomenon and doesn't have its eternal categories ready at the same time, and is not sufficiently cautious about saving mankind through saving each single individual into the race whatever the cost. The example is supposed to have had its effect on the child. One lets the child be a regular little angel, and then the depraved environment plunged it into depravity. Over and over again one is told how bad the environment was, and then, well then, the child became depraved. But if this happens in a simple quantitative process, then every concept comes to nothing. This is something people fail to notice. [Or] the child is made out to be so basically wicked that it derives no benefit at all from the good example. No doubt care is taken not to let the child become so wicked as to acquire the power to make fools not only of its parents but of all human speech and thought, just as the *rana paradoxa* [paradoxical frog][13] mocks and defies the naturalists' classification of frogs. There are many who indeed understand how to view the particular but are at the same time unable to keep the totality in mind. But whatever its other merits, every such view can only cause confusion. Or, the child, like most children, was neither good nor bad but then came into good company and became good, or into bad company and became bad. Middle terms! Middle terms! One comes up with a middle term that has the ambiguity which rescues the thought (and without it the salvation of the child is an illusion), namely, that the child, however its situation may have been, can become both guilty and innocent. Unless one has the middle terms prompt and clear, the concepts of hereditary sin, of sin, of race, and of the individual are lost, and the child with them.

———

Sensuousness then is not sinfulness, but through sin being posited and continuing to be posited, the sensuousness becomes sinfulness. That sinfulness means something else too goes without saying. But what else it signifies does not concern us here, where the task is to absorb oneself psychologically in the state that precedes sin.

Through eating the fruit of knowledge there entered the differentia between good and evil, but also the sexual difference as a drive. How this happened no science can explain. Psychology comes closest and explains the last approximation, which is freedom's showing-itself-for-itself in the anxiety of possibility, or in the nothing of possibility, or in the nothing of anxiety. If the object of anxiety is a something, we have no leap but a quantitative transition. The later individual has a "more" in relation to Adam, and again a more or less in relation to other individuals. But it remains true, regardless, that the object of anxiety is a nothing. If its object is something such that, when viewed essentially, that is, in terms of freedom, it signifies something, then we do not have a leap but a quantitative transition that confuses every concept. Even if I say that sensuousness for an individual prior to the leap is posited as sinfulness, it remains true that it is not essentially posited as such, for essentially the individual does not posit or understand it. Even if I say that a "more" of sensuousness is posited in the procreated individual, this in terms of the leap is nevertheless an invalid "more."

But if science should have any other psychological middle term that has the dogmatic, the ethical, and the psychological advantages possessed by anxiety, then that is what people prefer.

That in any case the present account lends itself excellently to the explanation commonly given of sin, namely, that it is selfishness, is easy to see. But by concentrating on that definition one does not engage the antecedent psychological difficulty at all, just as one also defines sin too pneumatically [spiritually][14] and takes too little note of the fact that, in being posited, sin posits just as much a sensuous as a spiritual consequence.

The fact that sin is so often explained in the newer sciences as selfishness makes it incomprehensible that no one has seen that just here lies the difficulty of finding a place for its explanation in any science. For selfishness is of all things the particular, and what this means is something only the single individual, as the single individual, can know, because when viewed under general categories it may mean everything in such a way that everything here means absolutely nothing. So this definition of sin as self-ishness may be quite right precisely when the additional claim is made that it is so empty of scientific content that it means nothing at all. Finally, in the definition of sin as selfishness, no account is taken of the distinction between sin and hereditary sin, along with the sense in which the one explains the other, sin explaining hereditary sin and hereditary sin explaining sin.

Once one begins talking scientifically about this selfishness, everything dissolves into tautology, or else one becomes clever and everything is confused. Who can forget that it was *Natur-philosophie* that found selfishness in all creation, found it in the movement of the stars which are nevertheless bound in obedi-ence to the laws of the universe, and found that the centrifu-gal force in nature is that of selfishness. If a concept has been widened that much, it may just as well lie down to sleep off its drunkenness and become sober again if it can. In this respect our age has been untiring in its efforts to make each thing signify everything. How cleverly and doggedly do we not see at times one or another mystagogue prostitute a whole mythology in order with his falcon eye to have every single myth become a caprice for his jew's harp? Cannot an entire Christian terminology sometimes be seen to degenerate into perdition at the hands of one or another speculator's pretentious treatment?

If one fails first to make clear to oneself the meaning of "self," it is of little use saying of sin that it is selfishness. But "self" sig-nifies precisely the contradiction of positing the universal as the particular. It is only given the concept of the particular that there can be talk of selfishness; but although there have lived countless millions of such "selves," no science can say what the self is without again stating it quite generally.* And this is the wonder of life, that each human being mindful of itself knows what no science knows, since one knows who one is oneself, and this is the deep meaning of the Greek saying γνῶθι σαυτόν [know yourself],†15 which has for too long been understood in the German way as pure self-consciousness, the airiness of idealism. It is high time we understood it in the Greek way, and then again as the Greeks would have understood it had they possessed Christian presuppositions. But the genuine "self" is posited only by the qualitative leap; there can be no question of it in the prior state. So when sin is explained in terms of selfishness, one gets entangled in indis-

*This is well worth further consideration, for here above all it must become apparent how far the recent principle that thought and being are one extends if one doesn't sprain it through misplaced and partly foolish misunderstandings, but also, on the other hand, doesn't want a highest principle bound up with thoughtlessness. Only the universal *is* by being thought, and lends itself to thought (not merely experimentally, for what can one not think?) and is as it lends itself to thought. The point in the particular is precisely its negative in-itself relation to the universal, its repellent relation, but as soon as it is thought away it is canceled, and no sooner is it thought than it is changed, so that either one does not think the particular but only imagines that one does so, or one thinks it and merely imagines that it is taken along in thought.

†The Latin saying *unum noris omnes* [if you know one, you know all] is a light-hearted expression of the same, and actually expresses the same, if by *unum* is understood the observer himself and one doesn't search inquisitively for an *omnes* but earnestly holds fast to the one that actually is all. In general, people don't believe this and it is even thought to be too proud. No doubt the real reason is that they are too cowardly and fond of ease to venture to understand and acquire an understanding of true pride.

tinct ideas, because it is, on the contrary, through sin and in sin that selfishness comes into being. If we are to say that selfishness occasioned Adam's sin, this explanation is a game in which the interpreter uncovers what he himself has first hidden. If selfishness is supposed to have brought about Adam's sin, the middle term is skipped over and the explanation has assured itself of a suspect facility.

Moreover, it tells us nothing about the significance of the sexual. Here I am back with my old point. Sexuality is not sinfulness; but, to speak foolishly for a moment and by way of accommodation, if Adam had not sinned, then the sexual would never have come into being as a drive. A perfect spirit cannot be conceived as sexually characterized. This also agrees with the teaching of the Church about the nature of the Resurrection,* with its representation of angels, and with the dogmatic definitions that have to do with Christ's person. Although, and just to throw a hint, Christ is tried in all human ordeals,† there is never any mention of temptation in this respect, which may be explained exactly by his having withstood all temptations.

Sensuousness is not sinfulness. Sensuousness in innocence is not sinfulness; nevertheless sensuousness is there. Adam did of course need food and drink, etc. The gender difference is posited in innocence but is not posited as such. Only in the instant that sin is posited is the gender difference also posited as a drive.

Here, as everywhere, I must decline every uncomprehending implication, as if, for instance, the true task were now to abstract from, that is, in an outward sense annihilate, the sexual. Once the

* [Cf. 1 Corinthians 15:45ff; Luke 30:34]
† [Cf. Hebrews 4:15]

sexual is posited as the extremity of the synthesis, all abstraction is of no avail. The task is of course to bring it under the attribute of spirit (here lie all the moral problems of the erotic). Realization of this is the victory of love in a person in whom spirit has so triumphed that the sexual is forgotten and recollected only in forgetfulness. When this happens, sensuousness is transfigured in spirit and anxiety is driven out.

If this view, whether we call it Christian or by any other name, is now compared with the Greek view, then I believe that more has been gained than lost. Doubtless we lose something of the plaintive erotic *Heiterkeit* [cheerfulness], but a spiritual category has also been gained that was unknown to Greek culture. Those who truly lose are the many who constantly live on as though 6,000 years had gone since sin entered the world, as if it were a curiosity that did not concern them. They do not gain the Greek *Heiterkeit*, which precisely cannot be *won* but only lost, nor do they gain the eternal attribute of spirit.

III

—

Anxiety as the Result of that Sin which is Sin-Consciousness's Nonappearance

The two previous chapters held consistently that the human being is a synthesis of soul and body, constituted and sustained by spirit. Anxiety was—to use a new expression that says the same as in the foregoing and also points to what follows—the instant in the individual life.

There is a category in constant use in recent philosophy, no less in logical inquiries than in those devoted to the philosophy of history. It is "transition." Yet no further clarification is ever forthcoming. The term is used without ceremony and while Hegel and the Hegelian school startled the world with that big thought, namely philosophy's presuppositionless beginning, or the thought that nothing must precede philosophy except everything's total presuppositionlessness, no embarrassment whatever is shown in using the terms "transition," "negation," "mediation," that is, the principles of motion in Hegelian thought, in a way that these do not also find their place in the systematic advance. If this is not a presupposition I do not know what a presupposition is. To help oneself to something that is nowhere explained is indeed to pre-

suppose it. The system is assumed to have such marvelous transparency and inner vision that it gazes with the omphalopsychite's[1]
immovability at the central nothing long enough for everything
to explain itself and its whole content to come into being of its
own. This introverted publicity was indeed that of the system.
Yet it proves not to be the case and, when it comes to its inner-
most agitations, the systematic thought seems to pay homage to
secrecy. Negation, transition, mediation are three masked and,
sinister secret agents (*agentia* [mainsprings]) that effectuate all
movement. Hegel would never call them hotheads, seeing that it
is with his most gracious permission that they carry on their ploy,
so unaffectedly that even logic uses terms and turns of phrase
borrowed from the temporal nature of transition: "thereupon,"
"when," "as being it is this," "as becoming it is that," etc.

Be that as it may, logic must be allowed to take care of itself.
The term "transition" in logic is and remains a conceit; it belongs
to the sphere of historical freedom, for transition is a *state* and is
actual.[*] Plato fully recognized the difficulty of introducing transition into pure metaphysics, which is why the category of *the
instant*[†] cost him so much effort. Ignoring the difficulty is cer-

---

[*] In saying that the transition from possibility to actuality is a κίνησις
[movement] Aristotle is therefore not to be understood logically but in
terms of historical freedom.

[†] Plato conceives of the instant purely abstractly. To orient oneself in its
dialectic, one should keep in mind that the instant is nonbeing under
the category of time. Nonbeing (το μὴ ὄν[that which is not], το κενον
[the empty] of the Pythagoreans [followers of the sixth-century BC
Ionian Greek philosopher famous for his wide application of mathemat-
ics and belief in the transmigration of souls]) occupied ancient as much
as it does modern philosophers. Among the Eleatics [pre-Socratic
fifth-century BC school founded by Parmenides in Elea] nonbeing was
conceived ontologically in such a way that what was affirmed of it could

be stated only in the contradiction that only being is. Pursuing this further one sees that it reappears in all spheres. In metaphysical propaedeutics the proposition was expressed as: He who expresses nonbeing says nothing at all (this misunderstanding is contested in the *Sophist,* and in a more mimetic manner already in an earlier dialogue, *Gorgias*). Finally, in the practical spheres, the Sophists used nonbeing as a means of canceling all moral concepts; nonbeing is not, *ergo* everything is true, *ergo* everything is good, *ergo* deceit and the rest simply do not occur. This position is contested by Socrates in several dialogues. Plato has dealt with it in the *Sophist* in particular, which like all his dialogues at the same time provides artistic illustration of what it teaches; for the Sophist, whose concept and definition the dialogue is looking for while dealing principally with nonbeing, is himself a nonbeing. Thus the concept and the example come into being at the same time in the war waged upon the Sophist, and which ends not with his annihilation but with his coming into being, which is all the worse for him, namely that here, despite his sophistry, which like the armor of Mars enables him to become invisible, he has to appear. Recent philosophy has come essentially no further at all in its conception of nonbeing, even though it presumes to be Christian. Greek philosophy and the modern alike maintain that everything turns on bringing nonbeing into being, since doing away with it or making it vanish seems so extremely easy. The Christian view has it that nonbeing is present everywhere as the nothing from which things were created as semblance and vanity [cf. Ecclesiastes 1:2], as sin, as sensuousness removed from spirit [cf. Romans 1:24, 28], as the temporal forgotten by the eternal [cf. 2 Thessalonians 1:9; Matthew 7:23, 25:12; Luke 13:25–27; John 3:18:36]; the task, consequently, is to do away with it in order to bring forth being. Only with this orientation in mind can the concept of Atonement be properly understood historically, that is, in the sense in which Christianity brought it into the world. If the term is understood in the opposite sense (the movement proceeding from the assumption that nonbeing is not), the Atonement is evaporated and turned inside out. It is in the *Parmenides* that Plato presents "the instant." This dialogue is occupied in pointing out contradictions within the concepts themselves, something that Socrates expressed so decisively that, while it reflects no discredit on the beautiful old Greek philosophy, it may well put a more recent and boastful philosophy to shame, one which, unlike the Greek, makes great demands not upon itself but upon people and their admiration. Socrates points out that there is nothing wonderful about being able to demonstrate the contradiction (τὸ ἐναντίον) in a particular thing participating in diversity, but if anyone could demonstrate contradictions in the concepts themselves, that would be something to admire (ἀλλ᾽ εἰ ὅ ἐστιν ἕν, αὐτὸ τοῦτο πολλά ἀποδείξει καὶ αὐ τα πολλά δὴ ἕν, τοῦτο ἤδη θαυμάσομαι, καὶ περὶ τῶν ἄλλων ἀπάντων ὡσαύτως, § 129b. [But if anyone can prove that what is simply unity itself is many or that plurality itself is one, then I shall begin to be astonished]). The procedure is however that of a dialectical thought experiment. It assumes both that the one (τὸ ἕν) is and that it is not, and then shows what follows from this for itself and for the rest. The instant now appears to be this strange entity (ἄτοπον [that which has no place], the Greek word is especially appropriate) lying between motion and rest without occupying any time, and into which and out of which that which is in motion goes over into rest and that which is at rest goes over into motion. Thus the instant becomes the category of transition (μεταβολή), for Plato shows that the instant is similarly related to the transition of the one to the many, of the many to the one, of likeness to unlikeness, etc., and that it is the instant in which there is neither ἕν [one] nor πολλά [many], neither differentiation nor combination (οὔτε διακρίνεται οὔτε ξυγκρίνεται §157a). Plato deserves credit for all this by making clear the difficulty, yet the moment remains a silent atomistic abstraction, which is not, however, explained by ignoring it. Now, if logic were willing to state that it does not have transition (and if it does possess this category, it must have its place within the system itself even if it also operates in the system), it would become clearer that the historical spheres and all the knowledge that rests on a historical presupposition do have the instant. This category is of great importance for blocking the way to pagan philosophy as well as an equally pagan speculation in Christianity. Another passage, in the *Parmenides*, points to the outcome of treating the instant as such an abstraction. Assuming the one to possess temporal attributes elicits the contradiction that the one (τὸ ἕν) becomes older and younger than itself and even the many (τα πολλά), and then again neither younger nor older than itself or than the many (§151e). The one must nevertheless be, so it is said, and "to be" is then defined as follows: Participation in an essence or a nature in the present time (τὸ δὲ εἶναι ἄλλο τι ἐστι ἢ μεθεξις οὐσίας μέτα χρόνου τοῦ παρόντος §151e). In explicating the contradiction further it then appears that the present (τὸ νῦν) wavers between meaning the present,

tainly not to "go further" than Plato; to ignore it, and to piously deceive thought in order to get speculation afloat and logic on the go, is to treat speculation as a somewhat finite affair. I remember, however, once hearing a speculator say that undue thought should not be spent on the difficulties that lie in the way, for then one will never come to speculate. If it is merely a matter of getting to the point of speculating, and not that one's speculation might actually be speculation, then indeed it is properly resolute to say that the important thing is to come to the point of speculating, just as for someone lacking the means to ride to the Deer Park in his own carriage it is praiseworthy of him to say: One should not bother with such things because one can just as well ride a shandrydan.[2] That is of course true. It is to be hoped that both riders arrive at the Deer Park. On the other hand, someone firmly resolved not to trouble himself over the means of conveyance just as long as he reaches the point of speculating will hardly come to speculate.

In the sphere of historical freedom, transition is a state. But to understand this properly one must not forget that what is new

---

the eternal, and the instant. This "now" (τo $\nu \hat{\upsilon} \nu$) lies between "was" and "will become," and "the one" cannot of course, in passing from the past to the future, leap over this "now." It comes to a halt *in* the now, does not become older but is older. In the most recent philosophy, the abstraction culminates in pure being, but pure being is the most abstract expression for eternity and is, in turn, as "nothing," precisely the instant. Here again we see how important the "instant" is, because only with it can one succeed in giving eternity its proper significance. Eternity and the instant become the extreme opposites, while dialectical sorcery otherwise contrives to make eternity and the instant mean the same. It is only with Christianity that sensuousness, temporality, and the instant are to be understood, because only here does eternity become essential.

comes about through the leap. If one does not insist on this, the transition will acquire a quantifying preponderance over the elasticity of the leap.

The human being was, then, a synthesis of soul and body, but also is a *synthesis of the temporal and the eternal*. That this has been said often enough I have no objection to, for it is not my wish to come upon novelties but rather my joy and dearest occupation to ponder over what appears quite simple.

As for this latter synthesis, what immediately strikes one is that it is formed otherwise than the first. The two factors there were soul and body, and then spirit the third, although in a way that one could properly speak of a synthesis only when spirit is posited. The latter synthesis has only two factors, the temporal and the eternal. Where here is the third? And if there is no third, then there is really no synthesis, for a synthesis that is a contradiction cannot be completed as a synthesis without a third, since the fact that the synthesis is a contradiction says exactly that it is not [a synthesis]. What, then, is the temporal?

If time is defined correctly as infinite succession, it may seem obvious that it should also be defined as present, past, and future. This distinction is, however, incorrect if considered as implicit in time itself, because the distinction arises only through the relation of time to eternity, and through eternity's reflection in time. If a foothold could be found in the infinite succession of time, that is, a present, which was the dividing point, then the division would be quite correct. However, precisely because every instant, as well as the sum of the instants, is a process (a passing by), no instant is a present, and in time there is accordingly neither a present nor a past nor a future. Thinking that this division can be upheld is due to an instant's being *spatialized,* but this brings the infinite succession to a halt; it is through introducing representation, by allowing time to be represented instead of being thought. But also this is to go about it incorrectly, for the infinite succession of time is an infinitely contentless present (this is the parody of the eternal) even for our powers of representation. The Indians speak of a line of kings that has ruled for 70,000 years. Nothing is known of the kings, not even their names (as I assume). Taking this as an example of time, the 70,000 years are an infinite vanishing. Representing it to ourselves is to expand and spatialize it into the illusory view of an infinite, contentless nothing.* On the other hand, once we let the one succeed the other, we are positing the present.

The present is not, however, a temporal concept except as something infinitely lacking content, which again is exactly the infinitely vanishing. Unless one watches out for this, no matter how quickly it disappears, the present will have been posited and having once posited it, one lets it find a place yet again in the categories: the past and the future.

The eternal is on the other hand the present. In thought, the eternal is the present in terms of an annulled succession (time was the succession that passes by). For what we can represent to ourselves, it is a going on that never moves from the spot, since for our powers of representation, the eternal is the infinitely contentful present. In the eternal there is again no division to be

---

*This incidentally is space. The practiced will see precisely in this a proof of the correctness of my presentation, because time and space are entirely identical (*nacheinander, nebeneinander*) for abstract thinking, become so for representation, and are truly so in the definition of God as *omnipresent* [cf. Psalms 139:7–12; Jeremiah 23:23–24; Acts of the Apostles 17: 24–27].

found into past and future, because the present is posited as the annulled succession.

Time, then, is the infinite succession; the life that is in time, and is only that of time, has no present. True, we are accustomed in defining the sensuous life to saying on occasion that it is in the instant and only in the instant. What is then understood by the instant is that abstraction from the eternal that, if it is to be the present, is its parody. The present is the eternal, or rather, the eternal is the present and the present is fullness. It was in this sense that the Latinist said of the deity that he is *praesens* (*praesentes dii* [the presence of the gods]), with which expression, applied to the deity, he also signified the deity's powerful support.

The instant signifies the present as a something that has no past and no future, for it is just in this that the imperfection of the sensuous life lies. The eternal, too, signifies the present, which has no past and no future, and this is the perfection of the eternal.

If one then wants to use the instant to define time and let the instant signify the purely abstract exclusion of the past and the future and as such the present, then the instant is not the present, since the intermediary between the past and the future, conceived purely abstractly, is not at all. But from this it can be seen that the instant is not just an attribute of time, because what characterizes time is only that it "passes by"; for which reason time, if it is to be defined by any of the attributes revealed in time itself, is time past. If, on the contrary, time and eternity touch each other, then it must be in time, and now we are with the instant.

"The instant" is a metaphor and in that regard not so good to deal with. But it is a beautiful word to take heed of. Nothing is as swift as a twinkling of the eye, and yet it is commensurable with the content of the eternal. Thus when Ingeborg looks out over the sea after Frithiof, this is a picture of the figurative expression's meaning.[3] An outburst of her feelings, a sigh or a word, has already as a sound more of time's definition, is present more in terms of vanishing and has in it less of the presence of the eternal; which is why a sigh, a word, etc., have the power to help the soul lighten itself of its burdensome weight, precisely because the burden, just by being expressed, begins already to belong in the past. A glance is therefore a designation of time, but mark well, of time in the fateful conflict when it is touched by eternity.* What we call the instant [or moment], Plato calls το ἐξαίφνης [the sudden]. Whatever its etymological explanation, it is related to the category of the invisible, with time and eternity being conceived equally abstractly because they lacked the concept of temporality, this again being due to their not having the concept of spirit. The Latin term is *momentum* (from *movere* [to move]), which by derivation expresses the merely vanishing.†

---

* It is remarkable that Greek art culminates in the plastic, which of all things lacks the glance. This however is deeply grounded in the fact that the Greeks did not understand the concept of spirit in the most profound sense, and nor therefore, in the most profound sense, sensuousness and temporality. What a striking contrast to Christianity, where God is pictorially represented as an eye.

† The New Testament has a poetic paraphrase of the instant. Paul says that the world will perish ἐν ἀτόμῳ και ἐν ριπῃ ὀφθαλμοῦ [in a moment and the twinkling of an eye; 1 Corinthians 15:52, where it is "we" that will perish]. In doing so he expresses the commensurability of the instant with eternity, due, that is, to the instant of destruction expressing eternity in the same instant. Let me illustrate what I mean, and forgive me if anything offensive should be found in the picture. Once here in Copenhagen there were two actors who probably never thought that their effort could have a deeper meaning. They stepped out onto the stage, placed themselves opposite each other, and then began miming one or another passionate conflict. When the act was in full swing

Understood in this way, the instant is not properly an atom of time but an atom of eternity. It is eternity's first reflection in time, its first attempt to as though bring time to a stop. This is why Greek culture did not understand the instant; for even if it understood the atom of eternity, it did not grasp that it was the instant, did not define it with a forward but with a backward direction, because for Greek culture the atom of eternity was essentially eternity, and so neither time nor eternity received what was properly its due.

The synthesis of the temporal and the eternal is not another synthesis but the expression for that first synthesis according to which man is a synthesis of soul and body sustained by spirit. Once spirit is posited, the instant is there. Which is why one may rightly say, reproachfully, of the human being that he lives only in the instant, since this occurs through an arbitrary abstraction. Nature does not lie in the instant.

As with sensuousness, so with temporality. For temporality seems still more imperfect, the instant less considerable than nature's seemingly secure subsistence in time. And yet the contrary is the case, nature's security has its ground in the fact that for nature time has no significance at all. Only in the instant does history begin. Through sin the human being's sensuousness is posited as sinfulness and is therefore lower than that of the beast, and yet this is precisely because this is where that which is higher begins. For now begins spirit.

The instant is that ambiguity in which time and eternity touch

---

and the spectator's eye followed the story in expectation of what would follow, they suddenly stopped and remained turned immovably to stone in their instantaneous mimical expression. The effect of this can be exceedingly comical, for the instant becomes accidentally commensurable with the eternal. The effect of the plasticity is due to the eternal expression being expressed eternally; the comic effect consists, on the other hand, in the eternalizing of something accidental.

each other, and with this the concept of *temporality* is posited, whereby time constantly intersects eternity and eternity constantly permeates time. Only now does the aforementioned division acquire its significance: the present time, the past time, the future time.

Attention is immediately drawn by this division to the fact that, in a sense, the future means more than the present and the past, because the future is in a sense the whole of which the past is a part, and the future can in a sense mean the whole. This is because the eternal means first the future, or because the future is the incognito in which the eternal, though incommensurable with time, wants nevertheless to preserve its commerce with time. Linguistic usage sometimes takes the future to be identical in this way with the eternal (the future life—life eternal). Since the Greeks did not have the concept of the eternal in any profound sense, neither did they have the concept of the future. Therefore one cannot reproach Greek life for being lost in the instant, or more correctly one cannot even say that Greek life was lost. For the Greeks conceived temporality just as naively as they did sensuousness, because the category of spirit was lacking.

The instant and the future in turn posit the past. If Greek life should in any way denote some temporal property, it is that of past time, not however defined in its relation to the present and the future, but as a property of time in general, as a passing by. This is where the meaning of the Platonic "recollection" comes to view.[4] For the Greeks the eternal lies behind, as the past that can only be entered in reverse.[*] It is an altogether abstract concept of the eternal nevertheless that thinks of it as the past, whether it

---

[*] One calls to mind here the category that I hold by, repetition, whereby one comes into eternity forward.

is further defined philosophically (a philosophical dying away) or historically.

One can, quite generally, in defining the concepts of the past, the future, and the eternal, see how one has defined the instant. If there is no instant, then the eternal appears behind as the past. It is as when I imagine a man walking along a road but do not posit the pacing, and the road then appears behind him as the distance covered. If the instant is posited but merely as a *discrimen* [division], then the future is the eternal. If the instant is posited, so is the eternal, but also the future which reappears as the past. This is clearly to be seen in the Greek, the Jewish, and the Christian views. The concept on which everything turns in Christianity, that which made all things new,* is the fullness of time,† but the fullness of time is the instant as the eternal, and yet this eternal is also the future and the past. If one doesn't watch out for this, not a single concept can be saved from a heretical and treasonable admixture that annihilates the concept. One then gets the past not by itself, but in a simple continuity with the future (the meaning of world history and the historical development of the individual thereby losing the concepts of conversion, atonement, and redemption). One gets the future not by itself, but in a simple continuity with the present (the concepts of resurrection and judgment being thereby laid in ruins).

Let us now imagine Adam and then remember that every later individual begins in the very same way but within the quantitative difference that results from the relations of generation and history. The instant is for Adam just as it is for every later individ-

* [2 Corinthians 5:17]
† [Galatians 4:4]

ual. The synthesis of the psychic and the somatic is to be posited
by spirit, but spirit is eternal and the synthesis *is* accordingly only
when spirit posits the first synthesis as, additionally, the second
synthesis of the temporal and the eternal. As long as the eternal
is not posited, the instant *is* not, or is only a *discrimen* [boundary].
The eternal, since spirit is in innocence only in the character of
dreaming spirit, appears thereby as the future, for this is, as has
been said, the first expression of the eternal, its incognito. Just
as (in the previous chapter) spirit, when it is about to be posited in the synthesis, or, more correctly, when it is about to posit
the synthesis as spirit's (freedom's) possibility in the individuality, expresses itself as anxiety, so too here does the future, the
eternal's (freedom's) possibility in the individuality. As freedom's
possibility manifests itself for freedom, freedom swoons and temporality now emerges in the same way as sensuousness in the
sense of sinfulness. I repeat here, again, that this is only the final
psychological expression for the final psychological approximation
to the qualitative leap. The difference between Adam and the later
individual is that the future is reflected more for the latter than
for Adam. This more, psychologically speaking, may well mean
something horrific, but in terms of the qualitative leap whatever
it signifies is inessential. The highest maximum of difference in
relation to Adam is that the future seems to be anticipated by the
past, or the anxiety that the possibility be lost before it was there.

The possible corresponds in all ways to the future. What is
possible for freedom is the future, and for time the future is the
possible. To both there corresponds anxiety in the individual life.
An accurate and correct linguistic usage therefore links anxiety
to the future. If one does indeed talk of being anxious about the
past, that seems to run counter to this usage. On more careful

examination, however, it appears that it is only a way of saying that the future manifests itself in some way or other. The past about which I am supposed to be anxious must stand to me in a relation of possibility. If I am anxious about a past misfortune, then it is not insofar as it is past but insofar as it may be repeated, that is, become future. If I am anxious because of a past offense, it is because I have not placed it in an essential relation to myself as past, but in some or other deceitful manner prevent it from being past. If it is actually past, then I cannot be anxious but only repentant. If I do not repent, then I must first let myself make my relation to the offense dialectical, but then the offense itself has become a possibility and not something past. If I am anxious about the punishment, it is only because this has been put in a dialectical relation to the offense (otherwise I suffer my punishment), and then I am anxious for the possible and the future.

We are thus back where we were in Chapter I. Anxiety is the psychological state that precedes sin, that comes as close as possible to it, as anxiously as possible, yet without explaining sin, which breaks out only in the qualitative leap.

The instant that sin is posited, temporality is sinfulness.* We

---

*From the definition of temporality as sinfulness it follows that death is in turn punishment [Romans 6:23; cf. 5:12]. This is an advancement whose analogue, *si placet* [if you please] may be found in the fact that, even regarding it as an external phenomenon, death announces itself the more terribly the greater the perfection of the organism. Thus while a plant's death and decay spread a fragrance almost more pleasing than its seasonal breath, the decay of an animal poisons the air. In a deeper sense it is indeed true that the more highly the human being is rated, the more frightful is death. The beast does not really die, but when spirit is posited as spirit, death appears terrifying. Death's anxiety therefore corresponds to the anxiety of birth, not that I would repeat on that account what has been said, partly truly and partly cleverly, partly enthusiasti-

do not say that temporality is sinfulness, any more than that sensuousness is sinfulness; but with the positing of sin, temporality signifies sinfulness. Therefore that person sins who lives only in the instant as abstracted from the eternal. But if, to allow myself to speak by way of accommodation and foolishly, Adam had not sinned, he would that very instant have passed over into eternity. On the other hand, as soon as sin is posited, it is no use wishing to abstract from the temporal, any more than from the sensuous.[*]

---

cally and partly frivolously, about death being a metamorphosis. In the moment of death the human being finds itself at the extreme point of the synthesis; it is as though spirit cannot be present for it cannot die, and yet it must wait because the body has to die. The pagan view of death was milder and more attractive, just as its sensuousness was more naïve, its temporality more carefree, but it lacked what is highest. One reads [Gotthold Ephraim] Lessing's beautiful treatise ["Wie die Alten den Tod gebildet. Eine Untersuchung" (1769)] on the representation of death in classical art, and cannot deny being moved with a sorrowful pleasure by the picture of this sleeping genius, or by seeing the beautiful solemnity with which the genius of death bows his head and extinguishes the torch. There is, if you will, something indescribably persuasive and alluring in trusting oneself to a guide like this, who is as conciliate as a memory in which nothing is remembered. But on the other hand there is also something sinister about following this silent guide, for he hides nothing, his form is no incognito. As he is, so is death, and with that everything is over. There is an unfathomable sorrow in this genius, with his friendly figure, bending down over the dying, and with the breath of his last kiss extinguishing the last spark of life, while little by little all that was experienced has already vanished, and death is left behind as the secret that, without being explained, explained that the whole of life was a game that ended with everything, great and small, going out like tapers, one by one, and last of all the soul itself, as the lighter. But then annihilation's muteness also lies there, in that it was all mere child's play and now the game is over.

[*] What has been explained here would also have been in place in Chapter I. I have nevertheless dealt with it here because it leads to what follows.

§1

The Anxiety of Spiritlessness

A look at life will quickly convince one that, if what has been presented here is correct, namely that anxiety is the last psychological state from which sin breaks out in the qualitative leap, then the whole of paganism and its repetition within Christianity rests in a merely quantitative categorization from which the qualitative leap of sin does not break out. This state is not however that of innocence but is, when viewed from the standpoint of spirit, precisely that of sinfulness.

It is quite remarkable that Christian orthodoxy has always taught that paganism rested in sin, whereas it was Christianity that first posited sin. Orthodoxy is however correct when it explains itself more precisely. Paganism as it were stretches out time with quantifying attributes, never arriving at sin in the most profound sense, but this precisely is sin.

That this is true in the case of paganism is easy to demonstrate. With paganism within Christianity it is another matter. The life of Christian paganism is neither guilty nor not guilty; it recognizes no real distinction between present, past, future, the eternal. Its life and history proceed as writing went over the paper in those old days with no punctuation marks but with one word, one sentence, rubbing shoulders with the other. From an aesthetic point of view this is extremely comical, for while it is beautiful to listen to a running brook murmur through life, it is nevertheless comical that a sum of rational creatures be transformed into a perpetual and meaningless muttering. Whether philosophy can use this *plebs* [multitude] as a category by letting it be the substratum for something greater, just as a vegetative mess gradually becomes solid earth, first peat and then more, I do not know. From the standpoint of spirit such an existence is sin, and the least one can do for it is to say so and demand spirit of it.

What is said here does not, however, apply to paganism. Such an existence can only be found within Christianity. The reason is that the greater the height at which spirit is posited, the more profound the exclusion appears; and the higher their loss, the more wretched in their contentment are οἱ ἀπηλγηκότες [those who are past feeling] (Eph. 4:19).* If the bliss of this spiritlessness is compared with the state of slaves in paganism, then there is some sense after all in slavery, because it is nothing at all in itself. The perdition of spiritlessness is on the other hand the most terrible thing of all, because the misfortune is precisely this, that spiritlessness has a relation to spirit, which is nothing. Spiritlessness may therefore possess in some degree the whole content of spirit, though mark well, not as spirit but as hobgoblins, gibberish, empty phrases, etc.; it may possess the truth, though mark well, not as truth but as rumor and old wives' tales. Looked at aesthetically, this is the deep comedy in spiritlessness, something not generally noticed since the presenter is himself more or less insecure in relation to spirit. So in staging spiritlessness one puts sheer prattle into the mouth of the actor, since one lacks the courage to put into the mouth of spiritlessness the same words one uses oneself. This is insecurity. Spiritlessness can say exactly the same as has been said by the most well-endowed spirit, but it does not say it in virtue of spirit. Qualified as spiritless, the human being has become a talking machine, and there is nothing

---

* [Ephesians 4:19; who "have lost all sensitivity"]

to prevent him from learning to repeat by rote a philosophical rigmarole, a confession of faith, and a political recitative. Is it not remarkable that the only ironist and the greatest humorist[5] had to join forces in saying what seems the simplest thing of all, namely, that a person must distinguish between what he does and does not understand? And what is to prevent the most spiritless human being from repeating the same thing verbatim? There is only one proof of spirit, and that is spirit's proof within oneself;* anyone demanding something else may chance on proofs in superabundance but is already to be defined as spiritless.

In spiritlessness there is no anxiety. It is too happy for that, too content, and too spiritless. But this is a very pitiable reason, and paganism differs from spiritlessness in the former being definable as directed *toward* spirit and the latter as directed *from* spirit. Paganism is, if you will, the absence of spirit and thus differs far from spiritlessness. Paganism is in this respect much to be preferred. Spiritlessness is spirit's stagnation and ideality's caricature. Spiritlessness is accordingly not literally dumb when it comes to repetition by rote, but it is *dumb* [has lost its sense] in the way in which it is said of salt that it has lost its flavor† and when one asks then how it can be salted. The perdition of spiritlessness, as well as its security, consists exactly in its understanding nothing in a spiritual way, seeing nothing as a task, even if with its clammy exhaustion it manages to fumble around everything. If it should on occasion be touched by spirit and begin for a moment to twitch like a galvanized frog,[6] we have a phenomenon corresponding perfectly to pagan fetishism. There is, for spiritlessness, no authority, for it

* [1 Corinthians 2:4]
† [Matthew 5:13:2: "if salt has lost its taste"]

does after all know that spirit lies under no authority; but since unfortunately it is not itself spirit, it is, despite this knowledge, a perfect idol-worshipper. It worships a dunce and a hero with the same veneration, but its real fetish is above all a charlatan.

Even if there is no anxiety in spiritlessness, because it is excluded just as is spirit, anxiety is still present except that it is waiting. Conceivably a debtor may be lucky enough to slip off from a creditor and hold him at bay with talk, but there is one creditor who never came off worst, namely, spirit. Seen from spirit's standpoint, anxiety is therefore also present in spiritlessness but hidden and masked. Even the observer shudders at the sight of it, because just as the figure of anxiety—if we allow ourselves to imagine such a shape—is frightful to look upon, its figure would terrify even more when it found it necessary to take on disguise in order not to appear as what it is, though being it no less. When death appears in its true form as the gaunt, grim reaper, one beholds it not without fright. But when, to mock those who fancy they can mock it, death appears in disguise, when the observer sees that the unknown figure captivating everyone with his courtesy and causing all to exult in the wild gaiety of desires is death, then a profound terror seizes him.

§2

Anxiety Dialectically Defined in Terms of Fate

It is commonly said of paganism that it rests in sin; it might be more correct to say that it rests in anxiety. Paganism is generally speaking sensuousness but a sensuousness that has a relation to spirit, although without spirit being in the most profound sense posited *as* spirit. But this possibility is precisely anxiety.

If we ask further what the object of anxiety is, then the answer must be that here as everywhere it is nothing. Anxiety and nothing always correspond to each other. As soon as the actuality of freedom and of spirit is posited, anxiety is canceled. But what is it then, more particularly, that the nothing of anxiety signifies in paganism? It is fate.

Fate is a relation to spirit as external to it; it is a relation between spirit and something other that is not spirit, and to which spirit nevertheless stands in a spiritual relation. Fate can mean just the opposite, since it is a unity of necessity and contingency. This is something not always remarked; there has been talk instead of the pagan *fatum* (with different modifications in the Oriental and Greek conceptions, respectively) as though it were necessity. A remnant of this necessity has been allowed to remain in the Christian view, in which it came to signify fate, that is, the contingent, that which is incommensurable in terms of providence. But that is not how it is. Fate is precisely the unity of necessity and contingency. This is cleverly expressed in the saying that fate is blind; for someone walking forward blindly does so as much by necessity as by accident. A necessity unaware of itself is, regarding the next instant, *eo ipso* [by that very fact] accidental. Fate, then, is anxiety's nothing. It is nothing because once spirit is posited, anxiety is canceled, but so too is fate, since providence is thereby also posited. Concerning fate, one can therefore say what Paul says about an idol: "no idol in the world really exists."* And yet the idol is an object of the pagan's religiousness.

In fate, then, the pagan's anxiety has its object, its nothing.

* [1 Corinthians 8:4]

The pagan cannot come into a relation to fate, because the very instant that it is the necessary, in the next it is the accidental. And still he is in relation to it, and this relation is the anxiety. Nearer to fate than this the pagan cannot come. Paganism's attempt to do so was profound enough to shed a new light on it. Whoever would explain fate must be just as ambiguous as fate itself. The *oracle* was that too. But then again, the oracle could mean just the opposite. So the pagan's relation to the oracle is once more anxiety. Here lies the profound and inexplicable tragedy of paganism. The tragedy lies however not in the ambiguity of the oracle's utterance, but in the pagan's not daring to forbear consulting it. He is in a relation to it, he dare not refrain from consulting it; in the very instant of consultation he is in an ambiguous relation to it (sympathetic and antipathetic). And then it is from here that one is supposed to reflect on the *oracle's* explanations!

The concept of guilt and sin in the most profound sense does not emerge in paganism. If it should emerge, paganism would have foundered upon the contradiction that one became guilty through fate. This is in fact the supreme contradiction, and it is in this contradiction that Christianity breaks forth. Paganism does not understand it, for that it is too frivolous in its definition of the concept of guilt.

The concept of sin and guilt posits the single individual precisely as the single individual. It is not a question of any relation to the world as a whole, to all of the past. It is a question only of the individual being guilty. And yet the individual is supposed to have become that through fate, that is to say, through all that of which there is no question, and is supposed thereby to have become something which precisely cancels the concept of fate, and it is through fate that the individual is supposed to become this.

This contradiction, if understood in the wrong way, provides

the misunderstood concept of hereditary sin, while rightly understood it provides the true concept, that is to say, the sense in
which every individual is both itself and the race, and the later
individual not essentially different from the first. In the possibility of anxiety, freedom sinks down, overcome by fate; freedom's
actuality now stands up with the explanation that it became
guilty. Anxiety at its most acute, where it is as though the individual became guilty, is not yet guilt. Sin comes, then, neither as a
necessity nor as an accident, and that is why that which answers
to the concept of sin is providence.

Within Christianity, one finds paganism's anxiety with regard
to fate wherever spirit, although present, is not essentially posited as spirit. The phenomenon is most evident when observing
a genius. In its immediacy, the genius as such is predominantly
subjectivity. Genius is not yet posited as spirit, for as spirit it can
be posited only by spirit. As immediate, it can be spirit (this is
what gives rise to the illusion that its extraordinary talent is spirit
posited by spirit), but then it has something else outside itself that
is not spirit and is itself in an external relation to spirit. That is
why the genius continually discovers fate, and the more profound
the genius, the more profound the discovery. To spiritlessness this
is of course foolishness, but in actuality it is greatness; for no one
is born with the idea of providence, and those who think that it
is acquired successively through upbringing are much mistaken,
even though I would not deny the importance of upbringing. It
is through its discovery of fate that genius shows its primordial
power, but then also in turn its impotence. To the immediate spirit,
which is what the genius always is, except that it is an immediate
spirit *sensu eminentiori* [in the eminent sense], fate is the limit.
Only in sin is providence posited. That is why the genius has an

enormous struggle in reaching it. If the genius does not reach it, then truly the genius becomes a subject for the study of fate.

Genius is an omnipotent *An-sich* [in-itself] which would, as such, shake the whole world. For the sake of order another figure therefore also appears, namely, fate. It is nothing. It is genius itself that discovers it, and the more profound the genius, the more profoundly discovered is the fate, since that figure is simply the anticipation of providence. If the genius continues to be merely a genius and turns outward, he will accomplish astonishing things, and yet he will always be subject to fate, if not outwardly and in a way tangible and visible to all, then inwardly. Therefore a genius-existence, when it does not turn to itself inwardly in the deepest sense, is always like an adventure story. The genius is capable of everything and yet dependent upon a triviality no one comprehends, a triviality upon which the genius through his own omnipotence bestows almighty meaning. That is why a second lieutenant, if a genius, is capable of becoming an emperor and changing the world, so that there becomes but one empire and one emperor. But for that reason, too, the army can be drawn up for battle, the conditions for battle be absolutely favorable, and yet in the next instant wasted; a kingdom of heroes may beg for the order for battle to be given—but no, he cannot: he must wait for the fourteenth of June. And why? Because that was the date of the battle of Marengo.[7] That is why everything can be in readiness, himself standing before the legions and waiting only for the sun to rise so as to proclaim silence for the oration that will electrify the soldiers. And the sun may rise more gloriously than ever, an inspiring and inflaming sight for all, only not for him, because the sun did not rise as gloriously as this at Austerlitz,[8] and only the sun of Austerlitz gives victory and inspires. Hence the inexplicable passion with which such a one may often rage against an entirely insignificant person, when otherwise he can show humanity and kindness even toward his enemies. Yes, woe unto that man, woe unto that woman, woe unto that innocent child, woe unto that beast of the field, woe unto that bird whose flight, woe unto the tree whose branch, comes in his way in that instant when he should take his warning.

Externals, as such, mean nothing to the genius, which is why no one can understand him. Everything depends upon how he understands them himself in the presence of his secret friend (fate). All may be lost; the simplest and the wisest unite in admonishing him not to undertake the fruitless venture. Yet the genius knows that he is stronger than the whole world provided that no doubtful commentary is found at this point in the invisible writing in which he reads the will of fate. If he reads it as he wishes, he says with his almighty voice to the captain of the ship, "Just sail on, you carry Caesar and his fortune."[9] All may be won, and that very instant he receives the intelligence, perhaps with a word the meaning of which no creature, not even God in heaven, understands (for, in a certain sense, God in heaven does not understand the genius), and with that the genius collapses in impotence.

Genius is thus placed outside the common run. It is great in its belief in fate whether it triumphs or falls, for it triumphs through itself and falls through itself, or rather, both are through fate. Commonly, its greatness is admired only when it conquers, and yet it is never greater than when falling by its own hand, fate here having to be understood as not proclaiming itself outwardly. When, however, in that very instant when humanly speaking all is won, he comes upon the doubtful reading and then collapses, one might well exclaim, "What a giant it would take to overthrow him."

But that is why no one was capable of doing so except himself. The belief that subdued the kingdoms and countries of the world under his mighty hand, while people believed they were witness to an adventure story, is the same belief that overthrew him, and his fall was an even more unfathomable tale of adventure.

Genius is therefore anxious at another time than are ordinary people. The latter first discover the danger in the moment of danger; until then they are secure, and when the danger has passed they are secure once again. In the moment of danger the genius is stronger than ever; his anxiety lies on the other hand in the moment before and the moment after, that moment of *frisson* when he must converse with the great unknown that is fate. His anxiety may be greatest precisely in the moment after, because the impatience of certitude always increases in inverse ratio to the brevity of distance, for there is ever more to lose the closer one comes to winning, and most of all in the moment of victory and because the consistency of fate is precisely inconsistency.

Genius as such cannot grasp itself religiously, comes therefore neither to sin nor to providence, and for that reason rests in the relation of anxiety to fate. No genius has ever existed without this anxiety unless he was also religious.

Genius, if it remains immediate in character and outwardly turned, will indeed become great and its exploits astounding; but it will never come to itself and never become great in its own eyes. All its activity is turned outward, and if I may so express it, the planetary nucleus from which everything radiates does not come about. The significance of genius for itself is none, or as questionably sorrowful as the sympathy with which the inhabitants of one of the Faroe Islands would rejoice if there lived on this island a native Faroese who astounded all of Europe through his writings in various European languages, and transformed the sciences through his immortal merits, but at the same time never wrote a single line in Faroese, and finally forgot how to speak it. To itself genius does not become significant in the most profound sense; its compass can extend no further than that of fate in relation to fortune, misfortune, esteem, honor, power, immortal fame, all of which are temporal terms. Every deeper dialectical characterization of anxiety is excluded. The ultimate would be to be considered guilty, so that anxiety is directed not toward guilt itself but toward its appearance, which is an attribute of honor. A state of the soul like this would lend itself nicely to poetic treatment. Such a state can happen to anyone, but the genius would straightaway grip it so deeply that he would be striving not with humanity but with the profoundest mysteries of human existence [*Tilværelse*].

It takes courage to understand that in spite of its splendor, glory, and significance, the existence of such a genius is sin, and one hardly comes to understand it before having learned to satisfy the hunger of the wishful soul. Yet that is how it is. That such an existence may be to some extent happy all the same proves nothing. One can certainly conceive one's talent as a means of recreation and realize, in so doing, that not for a moment does it rise above the categories in which temporality rests. Only through a religious reflection can genius and talent be justified in the deepest sense. To take a genius like Talleyrand,[10] there was in him the possibility of a much deeper reflection upon life. This he avoided. He pursued the defining trait in him that turned outward. His admired genius as an intriguer has been gloriously demonstrated; his resilience, the power of his genius to saturate (to use a term used by the chemists of corrosive acids) is admired, but he belongs to the temporal. If such a genius had scorned the temporal as being immediate, and had turned toward himself and toward the divine, what a religious genius would have come of it! But what agonies would he also have had to endure. To follow one's immediate traits is a relief in life, whether one is great or small; but the reward is also proportionate, whether one is great or small, and that person who is insufficiently mature spiritually to grasp that even immortal honor throughout all generations is merely a temporal attribute, that person who does not grasp that this, the striving for which keeps people's souls sleepless with desire and craving, is something very imperfect compared with the immortality that is for every person, and that would rightly arouse the justifiable envy of all the world if it were reserved for one person—that person will not come far in his explanation of spirit and immortality.

§3

Anxiety Dialectically in Terms of Guilt

It is commonly said that Judaism is the standpoint of the law. This could also be put in the following way: Judaism rests in anxiety. But here the nothing of anxiety signifies something other than fate; it is in this sphere that the phrase "be anxious of nothing" seems most paradoxical, for guilt is after all something. And yet it is true that as long as it is the object of anxiety, it is nothing. The ambiguity lies in the relation, for once guilt is posited, anxiety is gone and repentance is there. The relation, as always with that of anxiety, is sympathetic and antipathetic. This in turn seems paradoxical, yet it is not so, because while anxiety fears, it keeps up a subtle communication with its object, cannot look away from it, indeed will not; for if the individual does that, then repentance comes in. If this should strike someone as a hard saying, I cannot help him. Anyone with the required fixity to be, if I dare so put it, a divine prosecutor, if not in relation to others, then in relation to himself, will not find it hard. Moreover life offers phenomena enough in which, in anxiety, the individual gazes at guilt with something close to desire and yet fears it. Like the glance of the serpent, guilt has the power to fascinate. Here we find the truth in the Carpocratian view[11] that perfection is attained by way of sin. The truth in this lies in the instant of decision when the immediate spirit, yet through spirit, posits itself as spirit; it is blasphemy, on the other hand, to think it should be realized *in concreto*.

It is just here that Judaism is further advanced than Greek culture, and the sympathetic factor in its anxiety relation to guilt may also be recognized here by the fact that it would not at any price forgo this relation in order to acquire Greek culture's more reckless expressions: fate, fortune, misfortune.

The anxiety found in Judaism is anxiety about guilt. Guilt is a power that spreads itself everywhere and which, nevertheless, no one can understand in a deeper sense while it broods over human existence [*Tilværelse*]. Whatever is to explain it must therefore have the same character, in the same way that the oracle corresponds to fate. To the oracle in paganism there corresponds in Judaism the sacrifice. But that is why the sacrifice is something no one can comprehend. The profound tragedy of Judaism is analogous in this way to paganism's relation to the oracle. The Jew has recourse to the sacrifice but it does not help him, for what would really help is the canceling of the relation of anxiety to guilt and the positing of a relation that is actual. Since this does not happen, the sacrifice becomes ambiguous, which is expressed in its repetition, the further consequence of which would be a pure skepticism in terms of reflection upon the act of sacrifice itself.

So what applied in the foregoing, that it is only with sin that providence is there, holds good again here: only with sin is atonement posited, and its sacrifice is not repeated. The reason here is not in the, if I may so put it, outward perfection of the sacrifice; the perfection of the sacrifice corresponds to sin's actual relation being posited. Once the actual relation of sin is not posited, the sacrifice has to be repeated. (Thus the sacrifice is repeated in Catholicism although the absolute perfection of the sacrifice is still recognized.)

What has been briefly indicated here in world-historical terms repeats itself within Christianity in the individualities. Here again genius displays most clearly what lives in those less original in a way that is not so easily categorized. Broadly speaking, the only way in which genius differs from anyone else is in consciously beginning within its historical presupposition just as primitively as did Adam. Every time a genius is born, it is as though existence is put to a test; for genius runs through and experiences all that is past until it catches up with itself. Therefore the knowledge that genius has of the past is quite another than that offered in world-historical surveys.

That genius may remain immediate in its character has already been suggested, and the explanation that this is sin also contains what is the true courtesy shown to genius. Every human life is religiously arranged. Wanting to deny this confuses everything and cancels the concepts of individuality, race, and immortality. One could wish that people employed their acuity at this point, for here lie very hard problems. To say that someone with a mind for intrigue ought to be a diplomat or a plain-clothes detective, that someone with a mimetic talent for the comical ought to be an actor, and that someone with no talent at all ought to be a stoker in the courthouse, is an extremely fatuous way of looking at life, or rather it is not a way of looking at it at all, for it merely states the obvious. But explaining how my religious existence comes into relation with, and expresses itself in, my outward existence, that is the task. But who in our time bothers to think of things like that, even though life has at present more than ever the appearance of a transitory and fleeting moment? But instead of learning from this how to grasp the eternal, in chasing the moment one learns only how to pester oneself, one's neighbors, and the moment too, to death. If only one can join in, perform the moment's waltz just once, then one has lived, then one becomes the envy of those unfortunates who, though they were not born but tumbled headfirst into life and remain hurtling headlong onward, never reach it. Then one has lived, for what is more valuable in human life than a young woman's brief loveliness, which has indeed already held up uncommonly well if for just one night it has enchanted the dancers' ranks and faded first in the morning? There is no time to reflect how a religious existence pervades outward existence and interweaves it. Even if one does not pester with the hurry of despair, one still grabs hold of what is closest to hand. One may even become something great in the world. If then, on top of that, one attends church once in a while, then everything goes exceedingly well.

This seems to suggest that for some individuals the religious is the absolute, for others not,* and so "Goodnight!" to all meaning in

---

*With the Greeks the question of the religious could not arise in this way. It is however so wonderful to read what Plato tells in one place and makes use of. After Epimetheus [the brother of Prometheus] had fur-

life. The deliberation naturally becomes harder the more remote the outward task from the religious as such. What profound religious reflection would be required to stretch to such an outward task, for example, as that of becoming a comic actor? That it can be done I do not deny, for anyone with some understanding of the religious knows that this is more malleable than gold and absolutely commensurable. The fault of the Middle Ages was not religious reflection but that it came to a halt too soon. Here again we have the question of repetition: To what extent can an individuality, having once begun religious reflection, succeed in returning to itself whole, to the letter in every particular? In the Middle Ages they broke off. Thus when an individuality was to take hold of himself, having lighted once more upon the fact, for example, that he possessed wit, a sense of comedy, etc., he annihilated all of this as something imperfect. Today, this is all too readily considered foolish, since if someone has wit and a sense of comedy he is a fortune's Pamphilius;[12] what more could he wish? Such explanations contain, naturally, not the faintest presentiment of the problem, for as people nowadays are born more worldly wise than in older days, so too the greater number of them are born blind to the religious. We do nevertheless find examples also in the Middle Ages of this deliberation being carried further. Thus, for example, if a painter interpreted his talent religiously but it was not one that could express itself in achievements lying closest to the religious

---

nished man with all sorts of gifts, he asked Zeus whether he should hand out the ability to choose between good and evil in the same way that he had distributed the other gifts, so that the one received this ability while another received the gift of eloquence, and another that of poetry, and a third that of art. But Zeus replied that this ability should be distributed equally among all, because it belongs just as essentially to everyone alike.

sphere, an artist like this could no doubt be seen concentrating his mind on painting a Venus, interpreting his artistic calling just as piously as an artist who came to the aid of the Church by captivating the congregation's eyes with a vision of heavenly beauty. Nevertheless, with regard to all this, one has to wait for individuals to come forward who, despite outward gifts, do not choose the broad way* but rather the pain, the distress, and the anxiety in which they reflect religiously upon, and as though for a time lose, what it is surely only seductive to possess. Such a struggle is no doubt very exhausting, because there will be moments when they come close to regretting having started, and, yes, sorrowfully, perhaps sometimes almost to the point of despair, recall the smiling life that would have awaited them if they had followed the immediate urge of their talent. Yet, unquestionably, in the extreme dismay of distress, when it is as though all was lost because the way along which he would now push forward is impassable, and it is he himself who has cut off the smiling way of talent, the attentive person will hear a voice saying: Well done, my son! Just keep on, for he who loses all, gains all.†

We would now consider a religious genius, that is, one who does not remain in his immediacy. Whether he, at any time, turns himself outward remains for him a later question. The first thing he does is to turn toward himself. Just as the immediate genius has fate as the figure that follows him, so this one has guilt. In turning toward himself, he *eo ipso* turns toward God, and there is an established ceremonial rule that says that when the finite spirit would see God, then it must begin as guilty. In turning toward

* [Matthew 7:13–14]
† [Matthew 10:39]

himself, he discovers guilt. The greater the genius, the more profoundly is guilt discovered. The fact that for the spiritless this
should be folly is for me a delight and a joyful sign. The genius is
not like most people, and is not content with being so. The reason
is not that he disdains people; it is because primitively he has to
do with himself, while other people and their explanations are of
no help one way or the other.

That he discovers guilt so profoundly proves that this concept
is present to him *sensu eminentiori* [in the eminent sense], just
as is its opposite, innocence. That is how it was with the immediate genius's relation to fate, since everyone has a little relation
to fate, but then it stays there with the kind of empty talk that
is impervious to what Talleyrand discovered (and Young[13] had
already said), that the purpose of language is to conceal thoughts,
although not as effectively as empty talk does—which is to say,
conceal the fact that one has none.

In turning inward he discovers freedom. Fate he does not fear,
for he takes up no outward task and for him freedom is his bliss;
not freedom to do this or that in the world, to become king and
emperor or someone touting tickets for the age, but freedom to
know with himself that he is freedom. Yet the higher the individual rises, the greater the price to be paid for everything, and for
regularity's sake another figure takes shape with freedom's *An-sich*
[in-itself], namely, guilt. It is, as fate was, the only thing he fears,
and yet his fear is not what was its maximum in the former case,
namely, fear of being thought guilty, but fear of being guilty.

The more he discovers freedom, the more sin's anxiety is
upon him in the state of possibility. Only guilt frightens him,
for guilt alone can deprive him of freedom. That freedom here
is not at all defiance is easy to see, nor is it selfish freedom in

a finite sense. Attempts have frequently been made to explain the origin of sin by way of such an assumption. Such efforts are only wasted labor, since accepting such an assumption presents a greater difficulty than the explanation itself. When freedom is construed in this way, it has necessity as its opposite, which shows that freedom has been construed in terms of reflection.[14] No, the opposite of freedom is guilt, and that which is highest in freedom is its always having to do only with itself, projecting guilt in its possibility, and positing it accordingly through itself, and if guilt is actually posited, positing it through itself. If this is not borne in mind, freedom is cleverly confused with something entirely different, with *strength*.

When freedom now fears guilt, its fear is not in recognizing itself as guilty, if it is that, but rather in becoming so, for which reason freedom, as soon as guilt is posited, returns as repentance. But for the time being freedom's relation to guilt is a possibility. Genius manifests itself here again by not jumping aside from the primitive decision, not looking for the decision outside itself with Tom, Dick, and Harry, and not contenting itself with the usual haggling. Only through itself can freedom come to know whether freedom or guilt is posited. Therefore nothing is more ridiculous than assuming that the question of whether one is a sinner or guilty comes under the heading: lesson to be learned by heart.

The relation of freedom to guilt is anxiety, because freedom and guilt are still only possibility. However, as freedom with all its passion thus wishfully stares at itself and will hold guilt off so that not a speck of it might be found in freedom, it cannot refrain from staring at guilt, and this staring is anxiety's ambiguity, just as renunciation even within possibility is itself a coveting.

Here is where it now becomes clearly apparent in what sense there is a "more" in the anxiety of the later individual in relation to Adam's.* Guilt is a more concrete conception, which in the relation of possibility to freedom becomes ever more possible. It is in the end as though the guilt of the whole world united to make him guilty, and, what is the same, as though in becoming guilty he became guilty of the guilt of the whole world. Guilt, that is, has the dialectical character that it does not let itself be transferred to another account; whoever becomes guilty also becomes guilty of that which occasioned the guilt. For guilt never has an external occasion, and whoever yields to temptation is himself guilty of the temptation.†

In the situation of possibility this appears in the form of illusion; once repentance breaks forth with the actual sin, it has on the contrary the actual sin as its object. In freedom's possibility it is a matter of the deeper the discovery of guilt, the greater the genius, because the greatness of a human being depends simply and solely on the energy of the God relation in him, even if this God relation finds an altogether wrong expression as fate.

Just as fate finally captures the immediate genius, and this is indeed his culminating moment, not the glittering outward realization that causes amazement and even calls the craftsman from his daily occupation to stop and take notice, but the moment when, through himself, he collapses before himself, through fate, so too guilt captures the religious genius, and this is the moment of culmination, the moment when he is greatest, not when the sight of his piety is like the festivity of a special holiday, but when, through himself, he sinks down before himself in the depth of sin-consciousness.

---

* Yet it must not be forgotten that the analogy here is incorrect inasmuch as we are not dealing with innocence in the later individual but with repressed sin-consciousness.

† [James 1:14]

IV

—

Sin's Anxiety or Anxiety as the Outcome of Sin in the Single Individual

With the qualitative leap sin came into the world, and that is how it continues to come into it. You might think that once the leap was posited, anxiety was canceled, seeing that anxiety is defined as freedom's self-disclosure before itself in possibility. The qualitative leap is after all actuality, and possibility thus surely nullified along with anxiety. That, however, is not how it is. On the one hand, actuality is not a factor on its own; and on the other, the actuality posited is an unwarranted actuality. So anxiety enters into a relation again with what is posited, as well as with the future. But now the object of anxiety is something definite, its nothing an actual something, because the distinction between good and evil* is posited *in concreto*, and the anxiety has

* "What is the good?" is a question that comes ever closer to our time, since it is crucial in the question of the relationship among church, state, and morality. One must be cautious in giving an answer. Up to now the good has in an odd way been given preference because the trilogy of the beautiful, the good, and the true has been interpreted and presented in the sphere of the true (in knowledge). The good doesn't lend itself to definition. It is freedom. The difference between good and

therefore lost its dialectical ambiguity. This is true of Adam as of every later individual; for, through the qualitative leap, they are completely alike.

When sin is posited in the single individual through the qualitative leap, the difference between good and evil is then posited. We have nowhere committed the folly of holding that man *must*

---

evil comes to light only for and in freedom, and this difference is never *in abstracto* but only *in concreto*. Therefore, for those unseasoned in the Socratic method it is disturbing that he [Socrates] instantly brings this seemingly infinite abstraction, the good, down to what is most concrete. The method is entirely correct, except that he was mistaken (according to Greek thought he acted correctly) in interpreting good in its external aspect (the useful, the finitely teleological). Although the distinction between good and evil is freedom's, it is not so *in abstracto*. This misunderstanding arises because freedom is made into something else, into an object of thought. But freedom is never *in abstracto*. If freedom is given a moment to choose between good and evil, a moment when freedom itself is neither the one nor the other, then in that very moment freedom is not freedom but a meaningless reflection that the thought experiment serves only to confuse. If (*sic venia verbo* [pardon the expression]) freedom remains in the good, then it knows nothing at all of evil. In this sense one may say of God (don't blame me if anyone should misunderstand this) that he knows nothing of evil. By this I do not at all mean that evil is purely the negative, *das Aufzuhebende* [what is to be annulled] but on the contrary, that the fact that God knows nothing of evil, that he neither can nor will know anything about it, is the absolute punishment for evil. The preposition ἀπο [away] is used in this sense in the New Testament to signify removal from God or God's, if I dare so put it, ignoring of evil. If God is conceived finitely, it is indeed convenient for evil that God ignores it, but because God is the infinite, his ignoring it is its living annihilation. For the evil cannot dispense with God, even just to be the evil. I shall quote here a passage from Scripture, 2 Thess. 1:9, where it is said of those who do not know God and do not obey the gospel: οἵτινες δίκην τίσουσιν, ὄλεθρον αἰώνιον, ἀπὸ προσώπου του κυρίου, και ἀπὸ τῆς δόξης τῆς ἰσχύος αὐτοῦ [These will suffer the punishment of eternal destruction, separated from the presence of the Lord and from the glory of his might].

sin: we have, on the contrary, always protested against all merely thought-experimental knowledge. We have said what we again repeat, that sin presupposes itself just like freedom, and allows of no explanation through some antecedent, any more than does freedom. To maintain that freedom begins as a *liberum arbitrium* (which is found nowhere, cf. Leibniz), which can choose good just as well as evil, is to render any explanation fundamentally impossible. To speak of good and evil as the object of freedom is to finitize both freedom and the concepts of good and evil. Freedom is infinite and arises out of nothing. Wanting to say that man sins by necessity is therefore to construe the circle of the leap as a straight line. That to many such a procedure seems highly plausible is because to many thoughtlessness is the most natural thing of all, and to the fact that in all ages the number of those is legion who value the way of thinking that through all centuries has vainly been labeled λόγος ἀργός [lazy reasoning] (Chrysippus), *ignava rati* (Cicero), *sophisma pigrum, la raison paresseuse* (Leibniz).[1]

Psychology now has anxiety as its object once again, but it must be cautious. The individual's life history proceeds in a movement from state to state. Every state is posited by a leap. As sin came into the world, so does it continue to come unless halted. Yet every such repetition is not a simple consequence but a new leap. Preceding every such leap there goes a state as the closest psychological approximation. This state is the object of psychology. In every state possibility is present, and to that extent anxiety. Such is the case after sin is posited, for only in the good is there a unity of state and transition.

§1

Anxiety about the Evil

(a) Although the posited sin is an annulled possibility, it is also an actuality that lacks justification. That being so, anxiety is able to relate to it. As an unjustified actuality, it is again to be negated. That work anxiety is ready to undertake. Here is the playground for anxiety's artful sophistry. While sin's actuality holds one hand of freedom in its icy right hand, just like the Commandant,[2] the left hand gesticulates with illusion and deception and will-o'-the-wisp eloquence.*

(b) The posited sin is additionally consistent in itself, even if it is a consistency alien to freedom. This consistency announces itself, and anxiety's relation is to this consistency's future, which is a new state's possibility. No matter how deep the individual has sunk, it can sink still deeper, and this "can" is the object of anxiety. The more anxiety relaxes at this point, the more it signifies that sin's consistency has entered the individual *in succum et sanguinem* [in flesh and blood], and that sin has obtained native rights in individuality.

Sin here naturally means something concrete; one never sins on the whole or in general. Even the sin† of wanting to return to before sin's actuality is not a sin on the whole, and there never was such a sin. Anyone with some knowledge of human

---

* In view of the form of this investigation I can give only a quite brief summary and little more than algebraic hint as to the particular state. This is not the place for a proper description.

† This is said ethically, for ethics does not see the state but sees how the state is, in the same instant, a new sin.

beings recognizes very well the way in which sophistry constantly pounds away at only one particular point while the point is constantly changed. Anxiety wants the actuality of sin removed, not entirely but to a certain degree, or more exactly it wants to a certain degree to have the actuality of sin continue but, be it noted, only to a certain degree. Therefore it is not even against a little flirting with quantitative attributes, yes, the more developed anxiety, the further it dares to pursue this flirtation. But as soon as the jest and diversion of quantitative attributes come to the brink of catching the individual in the qualitative leap, which lies in wait like the larva of the ant lion[3] in the funnel formed in the loose sand, anxiety circumspectly withdraws. It then has a little point that must be saved and is without sin and the next instant another point. Consciousness of sin drafted profoundly and seriously in the diction of repentance is a great rarity. However, for my own as well as thought's and the neighbor's sake, I shall take good care not to put it as Schelling would probably have done. He speaks somewhere in the same breath of a genius for action and a musical, etc., genius.[4] It is sometimes possible in this way, without knowing it, to annihilate everything with a single word of explanation. Unless every person participates essentially in the absolute, it is all over. In the religious sphere, genius must therefore not be spoken of as a special gift bestowed upon only a few, for here the gift is that of willing, and whoever does not will should at least be shown the respect of not being pitied.

Sin, ethically speaking, is no state. The state is always, on the contrary, the last psychological approximation to the next state. Anxiety is now always present as the possibility of the new state. In the first state described under (a), anxiety is more noticeable, whereas in (b) it vanishes ever more from sight. But anxiety is still outside such an individual, and from the standpoint of spirit it is greater than any other anxiety. In (a), the anxiety is about the actuality of sin, out of which it sophistically produces the possibility, whereas looked at ethically it is sinning. The movement of anxiety is here the opposite of that of the anxiety of innocence, where, psychologically speaking, out of the possibility of sin it produces the actuality, whereas viewed ethically sin arises through the qualitative leap. In (b), anxiety is about the further possibility of sin. If anxiety decreases here, we explain it at this point through the triumph of the consistency of sin.

(c) The posited sin is an unjustified actuality; it is actuality, and posited by the individual as actuality in repentance, but repentance does not become the individual's freedom. In relation to sin, repentance is reduced to a possibility; in other words, repentance cannot cancel sin, it can only sorrow over it. Sin continues in its consistency, repentance follows it step by step, but always a moment too late. It forces itself to look at the horror, but like that mad Lear (*O du zertrümmert Meisterstück der Schöpfung!* [Oh thou ruined masterpiece of nature!])[5] it has lost the reins of government and retained only the power to grieve. Anxiety here is at its highest pitch. Repentance has lost its mind, and anxiety is potentiated to repentance. Sin's consistency goes onward, it drags the individual along like a woman dragged by the hair by an executioner while she screams in despair. Anxiety is ahead, it comes upon the consistency of sin before its arrival, as one can feel in one's bones that a storm is approaching. It comes closer; the individual trembles like a horse moaning as it halts at the place where it had once taken fright. Sin conquers. Anxiety throws itself despairingly into the arms of repentance. Repentance risks everything. It grasps sin's consistency as the pain of punishment, perdition as the consistency of sin. It is lost, its judgment has been pronounced, its condemnation certain, and the extra sentence for aggravated injury is that the individual be dragged through life to the place of execution. In other words, repentance has become deranged.

Life provides occasion to observe what is suggested here. Such a state is seldom found in altogether corrupt natures, generally only among the more profound. For it takes considerable primitivity as well as a manic persistence of will not to fall under (a) or (b). No dialectic is capable of defeating the sophism that a deranged repentance manages at every moment to come up with. A repentance like that has a contriteness that in the dialectic and expression of passion is far more powerful than true repentance. (In another sense it is of course more impotent, yet, no doubt as anyone who has observed such a case has noticed, it is remarkable what persuasive talent and what eloquence such a repentance possesses for disarming all objections and convincing all who come close, only to despair of itself again when this, its diversion, is over.) Trying to stop this horror with words and phrases is wasted effort, and whoever contemplates doing so can always be sure that his sermonizing will be like the babble of children compared with the elemental eloquence at the service of such a one. The phenomenon can appear in connection as much with the human's sensuous side (addiction to drink, to opium, or to debauchery, etc.) as with the more elevated (pride, vanity, wrath, hatred, defiance, subtlety, envy, etc.). The individual may repent of its wrath, and the profounder the individual, the profounder the repentance. But repentance cannot make the individual free. There the individual is mistaken. The occasion arrives, anxiety has already discovered it, every thought quivers, anxiety sucks the blood from the powers of repentance and shakes its head. It is as if wrath had already triumphed, the individual has already an uneasy feeling of the prostration of freedom that is reserved for the next moment. The moment comes. Wrath triumphs.

Whatever sin's consistency, the fact that the phenomenon appears on a respectable scale is always the sign of a deeper nature. That it is seen fairly seldom in life, that is to say, that one has to be an observer to see it more often, is because it can be concealed and also often expelled insofar as one or another precautionary measure is used to abort this, the embryo of the highest life. You need only seek the advice of Tom, Dick, and Harry to become as most people are, and you will always be able to secure the judgment of a few respectable people that this is just what you are. The best proved way to escape spiritual trial is to become spiritless and the sooner the better. Everything, if only taken care of in time, takes care of itself. And as for spiritual trial, one can explain that there is no such thing, or that it can at most be considered a piquant poetical fiction. In days of old, the road to perfection was narrow and solitary, the journey down it always disturbed by aberrations, exposure to sin's predatory attacks, and pursuit by the arrow of the past, which is as perilous as that of the Scythian hordes.[6] Now one travels to perfection in good company on the railroad and has arrived before one knows it.

All that can truly disarm the sophism of repentance is faith, courage to believe that the state itself is a new sin, courage without anxiety to renounce anxiety, something of which only faith is capable; not that it therefore annihilates anxiety, but, eternally young itself, it extricates itself from anxiety's moment of death. Only faith is capable of doing this, for only in faith is the synthesis eternally and in every instant possible.

It is not difficult to see that everything presented here belongs to psychology. Ethically, everything depends on getting the individual rightly positioned in relation to sin. Once there, the individual stands repentant in its sin. Looked at in terms of the idea,[7] the individual has that very instant fallen into the hands of dogmatics. Repentance is the highest ethical contradiction, partly because by demanding ideality it has to content itself with accepting repentance, partly because repentance is dialectically ambiguous regarding what it is to cancel, an ambiguity that dogmatics cancels only in the Atonement, in which the category of hereditary sin becomes clear. Moreover repentance delays action, and action is precisely what ethics demands. Finally, repentance must become an object to itself, seeing that the moment of repentance becomes a deficit of action. It was therefore an authentically ethical exclamation, full of energy and courage, when the elder Fichte[8] said there was no time to repent. In saying it, however, he did not bring repentance to its dialectical extreme, where, posited, it will nullify itself through new repentance, and where it then collapses.

What has been expounded in this section, as everywhere in this work, is what psychologically can be called freedom's psychological attitudes toward sin, or sin's psychological, approximating states. These do not presume to explain sin ethically.

§2

Anxiety about the Good (the Demonic)

Today one rarely hears talk of the demonic. The single narratives* about it in the New Testament are usually put aside. Insofar as they seek to explain them, theologians usually get lost in observations on one or another unnatural sin, among which are also found examples of the bestial having so far gained the upper hand in a person as to declare itself in inarticulate animal noises, a bestial expression, and a brutish glance, whether it means that the animality has acquired a pronounced form in the person (the physiognomic expression—Lavater)[9] or is seen just in glimpses like a disappearing express messenger, suggesting what dwells within, in the same way as in an instant shorter than the shortest instant the glance or gesture of the insane parodies, ridicules, and jeers at, the rational, self-possessed and clever man together with whom he stands and talks. What theologians say in this respect may be quite true, but it all depends on what the point is. The way in which the phenomenon is usually described makes it clear that what they are talking about is the bondage of sin, the state that I know no better way of describing than by recalling a game in which two persons are concealed under one cloak as though there were only one, and the one speaks while the other gesticulates in a way that is quite arbitrary in relation to what is said. For this is how the beast has taken on human form and now constantly jeers at him with his gesticulations and byplay. But the

* [Cf. Matthew 8:28–34, 9:32–34, 12:22–32, 17:14–18; Mark 1:23–28; John 10:20–21]

bondage of sin is not yet the demonic. Once sin is posited, and the individual continues in sin, there are two formations, one of which is described in the foregoing section. Unless one attends to this, the demonic cannot be identified. The individual is in sin, and his anxiety is about the evil. This formation, when seen from a higher standpoint, is in the good, for that is why it is anxiety about the evil. The other formation is the demonic. The individual is in the evil and is anxious about the good. The bondage of sin* is an unfree relation to the evil, but the demonic is an unfree relation to the good.

The demonic therefore first comes clearly in sight only when it is touched by the good, which now comes to its boundary from outside. This is why it is noticeable that the demonic in the New Testament first appears with Christ's arrival, and, whether the demon is a legion (cf. Matthew 8:27–34;† Mark 5:1–20; Luke 8:26–39) or is dumb (cf. Luke 11:14), the phenomenon is the same, namely, anxiety about the good, for anxiety can just as well express itself in muteness as with a scream. The good, of course, signifies the restoration of freedom, redemption, salvation, or whatever one wants to call it.

In earlier times there has often been talk of the demonic. There is no point here in making or having made studies that would put one in a position to recite from or cite learned and abstruse books. It is easy to sketch the different views that are possible and have been topical at various times. This can be important, because the difference in these views can show the way toward a definition of the concept.

* [Cf. John 8:34]
† [Properly Matthew 8:28–34]

The demonic can be viewed from an aesthetic-metaphysical point of view. The phenomenon will then come under the heading of misfortune, fate, etc., and be viewed as analogous to congenital mental disorder, etc. This is to approach the phenomenon sympathetically, but just as wishing is the most paltry of all solo performances, so too, in the way the word is usually taken, is being sympathetic the most paltry of all social virtuosities and aptitudes. Far from standing the sufferer in good stead, sympathy is sooner just a way of protecting one's own egotism. Not daring in a deeper sense to think about such things, one saves oneself through sympathy. It is only when the sympathetic person relates in his compassion to the sufferer in a way that he understands, in the strictest sense, that it is his own case that is in question, only when he knows how to identify himself with the sufferer in a way that, in struggling for an explanation, he is struggling for himself, renouncing all thoughtlessness, soft-heartedness, and cowardice, it is only then that the sympathy acquires meaning, and perhaps only makes sense when the sympathizer differs from the sufferer in suffering under a higher form. When sympathy relates in this way to the demonic, it will not be a matter of some few words of comfort or a pittance or a shrug of the shoulder; for someone who groans has something to groan about. If the demonic is a fate, then it can happen to anyone. There is no denying this, even if in our cowardly age everything possible is done by way of diversions and the brass band of loud enterprises to keep lonely thoughts at bay, just as in the American forests wild beasts are kept off with torches, shouting, and the beating of cymbals. This is why today people learn so little about the highest spiritual trials but all the more about those cringing conflicts between man and man, and between man and woman, that a refined society- and soirée-life brings with it. If true human sympathy is to have suffering as its guarantor and surety, then it must first become clear about to what extent it is fate and to what extent guilt. And this distinction must be drawn up with the troubled but also energetic passion of freedom, so that a person dares hold fast to it though the whole world collapses, though it might seem that, through his own firmness, he brought about irreparable harm.

The demonic has been viewed in ethically condemnatory terms. The frightful severity with which it has been pursued, identified, and punished is well known. In our time we shudder at these accounts, and we become sentimental and emotional at the thought that in our enlightened age we do not act in that way. That may well be so, but is sentimental sympathy all that more praiseworthy? Here it is not for me to judge or condemn that behavior, only to observe it. The very fact that ethically it was so severe shows that its sympathy was of a better quality. Identifying itself in thought with the phenomenon, it had no further explanation than that the phenomenon was guilt. It was therefore convinced that when all is said and done, the demoniac, according to his better possibility, should wish for all the cruelty and severity to be employed against him.* Was it not, to take an example from a similar sphere, Augustine who recommended punishment, even the death penalty,[10] for heretics? Was that because he lacked sympathy? Or was it not rather that his behavior differed from that of

---

*The person who is not so ethically developed as to feel comfort and relief, even when he suffers the most, if another had the courage to say to him, "This is not fate, it is guilt," and said it sincerely and earnestly, is not ethically developed in a big sense, because the ethical individuality fears nothing as much as fate and some aesthetic jangle which, under the cloak of compassion, would trick him out of the gem that is freedom.

our own time because his sympathy had not made him cowardly, so that of himself he would have said: God grant that if it should come to that with me, there would be a Church that did not abandon me but would use all its power. In our day, however, people are, as Socrates somewhere says, afraid of letting themselves be cut and cauterized by the physician in order to be healed.

The demonic has been viewed in terms of medical treatment. And, it goes without saying, *mit pulver und mit pillen* [with powder and with pills] and then with enemas! The pharmacist and the doctor now got together. The patient was isolated so as not to put fear into others. In our brave time we dare not tell a patient he is about to die, we dare not call the pastor in case the patient should die of fright, and we dare not tell the patient that just recently someone died from the same illness. The patient was isolated, sympathy made inquiries after him, the physician promised to issue a report as soon as possible and a statistical survey so as to determine the average. And when you have an average, all is explained. The medical-treatment view regards the phenomenon as purely physical and somatic, and as physicians often do, *in specie* [in particular] in one of Hoffmann's short stories, he takes a pinch of snuff and says: It is a critical case.[11]

That three so differing views are possible shows the ambiguity of the phenomenon and indicates that it belongs in a way to all spheres: the somatic, the psychic, and the spiritual [*pneumatisk*]. This suggests that the demonic has a much larger compass than is commonly assumed, which can be explained by the fact that the human being is a synthesis of psyche and soma sustained by spirit, and a disorder in one therefore manifests itself in the others. But when one is first aware of the broad scope of the demonic, it will perhaps become clear that many even of those who wish to deal with this phenomenon come themselves under its category, and that there are traces of it in every person as surely as every person is a sinner.

But because the demonic has in the course of time meant all manner of things, and has come in the end to mean anything you please, the best course is to define it a little. For this, attention should be paid to the place we have already assigned it. In innocence there can be no question of the demonic. On the other hand, all fantasies of entering into a pact with evil, etc., in which a person becomes totally evil, must be abandoned. It was from this that the contradiction in that strict behavior of earlier times arose. The assumption [of total evil] was made and yet one still wanted to punish. The punishment itself was not just self-defense, it was also intended to save (either through a milder punishment for the one involved or by way of capital punishment for others). But then if there could be talk of salvation, the individual was not entirely in the grip of evil, while if the individual were entirely in the grip of evil, then punishment would be a contradiction. If the question should arise here as to how far the demonic is a problem for psychology, I would have to reply, the demonic is a state. Out of this state, the particular sinful act can constantly break forth. But the state is a possibility, although again, of course, in relation to innocence it is an actuality posited through the qualitative leap.

The demonic is anxiety about the good. In innocence, freedom was not posited as freedom; its possibility in the individual was anxiety. In the demonic the relation is reversed. Freedom is posited as unfreedom, because freedom is lost. Here again freedom's possibility is anxiety. The difference is absolute, because freedom's possibility appears here in relation to unfreedom, which is the very opposite of innocence, that being an attribute directed toward freedom.

The demonic is unfreedom that wants to close itself off. This is and remains, however, an impossibility; it retains always a relation, and even when this appears to have altogether disappeared, it is still there and anxiety immediately manifests itself in the instant of contact (see what is said above of the accounts in the New Testament).

The demonic is *the reserved and the involuntarily disclosed.* The two definitions indicate the same thing, as also they should, because the reserved is precisely the mute, and if the latter has to express itself, it must do so against its will, seeing that the freedom that lies in unfreedom's ground, by entering into communication with freedom from the outside, revolts and now betrays unfreedom in a way that means that it is the individual that betrays itself against its will in anxiety. Being reserved must therefore be taken in a very distinct sense, for as commonly used, the term may signify the greatest freedom. Brutus, Henry V of England as Prince of Wales,[12] etc., were confirmed in the isolation of their reserve in this sense until such time as it became evident that their reserve was a pact with the good. A reserve of this kind was therefore identical with an expansiveness, and never was there a reserved individuality more beautiful and noble in its expansiveness than one whose isolation is in the womb of a great idea. For freedom is precisely the expansive. As against this, what I mean here is that reserve κατ' ἐξοχήν [in an eminent sense] can be used about unfreedom. Usually a more metaphysical expression is used for evil, that it is denial. Its ethical expression, when the effect is observed in the individual, is precisely this reserve. The demonic does not reserve something *to* itself but reserves itself, and the profundity of human existence [*Tilværelse*] rests precisely in this, that unfreedom takes itself captive. Freedom is always in communication (even taking the religious meaning of the word[13] into consideration does no harm); unfreedom withdraws ever more in its reserve and will not communicate. This can be seen in all spheres. It appears in the hypochondriac, the fantast; it appears in the greatest passions when in a profound misunderstanding these bring on the silent treatment.* When freedom now touches reserve, it becomes anxious. Of a person there is in common speech a very suggestive saying: "He won't come out with it."[14] Reserve is precisely muteness. Language, the word, is precisely what saves, saves from the empty abstraction of reserve. Let x signify the demonic, the relation of freedom to it something outside; the law for the disclosure of the demonic is that it "comes out with it" against its will. For language implies communication. Therefore a demoniac in the New Testament says to Christ, when he approaches: τί έμοὶ καὶ σοὶ [What have I to do with you], and goes on to suggest that Christ has come to destroy him (anxiety about the good).† Or a demoniac implores Christ to go another way. (When anxiety is about evil, see §1, the individual then resorts to salvation.)

Life is rich in examples of this in every possible sphere and to all possible degrees. A hardened criminal will not confess (here

---

* It has already been said, and is said here again, that the demonic has a scope quite other than is generally believed. The preceding section indicated the formations pointing in the other direction. Here follows the second series of formations, and the distinction can be carried through in the way I have presented it. If something better can be offered, one should choose that but at least exercise caution in this area, otherwise everything runs together.

† [Mark 5:6–7; Mark 1:23–24]

the demonic lies in his not wanting to communicate with the good by suffering the punishment). There is a procedure, perhaps not so often employed, that can be applied in such cases. It is silence and the power of the eye. If an interrogator has the physical endurance and spiritual elasticity to keep going without moving a muscle for as much as sixteen hours, he will succeed and the confession will burst out involuntarily. No person with a bad conscience can endure silence. Placed in solitary confinement he becomes apathetic, but this silence in the presence of the judge, with the clerks waiting to inscribe everything in the protocol, is itself the most acute and searching question, the most frightful torture and yet permitted although not at all as easy to accomplish as might be supposed. The only thing that can get reserve to speak is either a higher demon (for every devil has his day)[15] or the good that can keep absolutely silent. And should any ingenious attempt be made to embarrass this examination-by-silence, it is the interrogator himself who will be brought to shame, and in the end it will be he that becomes afraid of himself and has to break the silence. In the face of a subordinate demon and subordinate human natures, whose consciousness of God is not well developed, reserve triumphs unconditionally, because the former cannot hold out and the latter are in all innocence accustomed to live from hand to mouth and with their hearts on the tips of their tongues.[16] It is incredible what power the reserved can wield over such people, how these beg at last and plead for just a word to break the silence; but it is also shocking to tread the weak underfoot in this manner. One might think that such things occur only among princes and Jesuits, and that to get a clear idea of this one must think of Domitian, Cromwell, Alba, or a general of the Jesuit order,[17] whose names have become almost common nouns for this. Not at all. It occurs far more frequently. However, one should be cautious in judging the phenomenon, for although as a phenomenon it is the same, the reason for it may be quite the opposite; an individuality who exercises reserve's despotism and torture might himself wish to speak, and might himself wait for a higher demon who could bring the revelation forth. However, a tormenting reserve may also relate selfishly to its reserve. On this subject I could write a whole book, even though I have not been, as is the custom and the established convention among the observers of our day, in Paris and London, as if one could acquire in this way such great learning other than chatter and the wisdom of traveling salesmen. If only one pays attention to oneself, one has as an observer enough with five men, five women, and ten children for the discovery of all possible states of the human soul. What I would have to say might also be of some importance especially for everyone who deals with children or has any relation to them. It is infinitely important that the child be lifted up through a presentation of exalted reserve and rescued from the misunderstood kind. Externally, it is easy to see when the moment arrives when one dares to let the child go alone; in a spiritual respect it is not so easy. In a spiritual respect, the exercise is very difficult and one cannot escape taking it upon oneself by employing a nursemaid or buying a walking chair.[18] The art is to be constantly present and yet not present, so that the child is allowed to develop itself, while at the same time keeping a clear overview. The art is, to the very highest degree and on the greatest possible scale, to leave the child to itself and to express this apparent abandonment in a way that one keeps up with everything without being noticed. Time for this can well be found, even if you are a royal functionary, if only one will. Everything can be done if one will. And the father or the educator who has done everything else for the one to whom care is entrusted but has not prevented the child from becoming reserved has always incurred a great liability.

The demonic is the reserved, the demonic is anxiety about the good. Let the reserve be *x* and its content *x*, be it the most terrible and the most trivial, the most awful thing whose presence in life not many may dream of, but also the trifles to which no one pays attention.* What then does the good mean as *x*? It means disclosure.† Disclosure may in turn mean the highest (redemption in an eminent sense) as well as the least significant (an accidental remark). This must not distract us, for the category remains the same, the phenomena having this in common, that they are demonic even if the difference is otherwise dizzying. Disclosure here is the good, for disclosure is the first expression of salvation. That is why we have an old saying that if only one dare say the word, the sorcerer's spell is broken, and that is why the somnambulist wakes up when one mentions his name.

* Being able to use one's category is a *conditio sine qua non* [indispensable condition] if observation is to have any deeper meaning. When the phenomenon is present to some degree, most people will take note of it but be unable to explain it because they lack the category; and if they did have it, they would have a key to open up any trace of the phenomenon wherever it occurs, for the phenomena within the category obey it as the spirits of the ring obey the ring [*Aladdin, A Thousand and One Nights*].

† I have purposely used the word "disclosure." Here I might also have called the good "transparency." If I thought that the word "disclosure," and the development of its relation to the demonic, might be misunderstood as though always having to do with something external, a palpably transparent confessional but which in being external was of no help, I would certainly have chosen another word.

The collisions of reserve regarding disclosure can again be infinitely varied, with innumerable nuances, because the exuberant growth of the spiritual life is not inferior to that of nature, and the varieties of the spiritual states are more innumerable than those of the flowers. Reserve may wish for disclosure, wish that this be brought about from the outside, that it might happen to it. (This is a misunderstanding, for it is a womanly relation to the freedom posited in disclosure, and to the freedom that posits disclosure; unfreedom may still therefore remain even if the reserved person's state is one of greater happiness.) Reserve may will disclosure to a degree but still retain a little residue of itself in order to begin the reserve all over again. (This is the case with subordinate spirits, who can do nothing *en gros* [wholesale].) It can will disclosure but *incognito*. (This is reserve's subtle contradiction, examples of which are found in the lives of poets.) Disclosure may already have triumphed, but in the same instant reserve risks the last attempt and is ingenious enough to transform the disclosure itself into a mystification, and reserve has triumphed.*

However I dare not continue further, for how could I ever finish giving names even algebraically, let alone were I to give descriptions, were I to break reserve's silence and let its monologues become audible, for the monologue is precisely its speech, and that is why in describing a reserved person we say that he talks to himself. So here I shall try only to give *"allem einen Sinn,*

---

* It is easy to see that reserve *eo ipso* means lying, or if you will, untruth. But untruth is precisely unfreedom, which is anxious about disclosure. That is why the devil is called the father of lies [John 8:44]. That there is a big difference between lie and untruth, between lie and lie, and between untruth and untruth, I have indeed always admitted, but the category is the same.

aber keine Zunge [all an understanding but no tongue]," as the reserved Hamlet admonishes his two friends.[19]

I shall however hint at a collision in which the contradiction is as terrible as reserve itself. What the reserved person in his reserve conceals can be so terrible that he dare not utter it, not even to himself, because it is as though in the very utterance he committed a new sin, or as if it tempted him again. For this phenomenon to occur, the individual must be a rare mixture of purity and impurity. That is why it is most likely to occur when, having done something horrific, the individual has lost self-control. Someone in a drunken state may similarly have done what he only dimly recalls, yet know that it was so wild that he can scarcely recognize himself. The same may also occur with someone who was once insane and retains a memory of the former state. What decides whether the phenomenon is demonic is the individual's attitude toward disclosure, whether the individual will interpenetrate that fact with freedom, accept it in freedom. Once he will not do this, the phenomenon is demonic. This must be kept clearly in mind, for even the person who will do it is essentially demonic. He has, that is to say, two wills, one subordinate, impotent, that wills revelation and a stronger that wills reserve, but the fact that this will is the stronger indicates that essentially he is demonic.

Reserve is involuntary disclosure. The weaker the individuality in its primitivity, or the more the elasticity of freedom is eaten away in the service of reserve, the more likely it is that the secret will finally break out. The slightest touch, a passing glance, etc., is enough for that horrific or—depending on the content of the reserve—comic ventriloquism to make its start. The ventriloquism itself may be plainly declarative or indirect, as when some insane person betrays his insanity by pointing to another person and says: I can't stand him, he must be mad. The disclosure may declare itself in words, as when the unhappy man ends by thrusting his hidden secret upon everyone. It may declare itself in facial expression, a glance, because there are looks in which a person involuntarily reveals what is hidden. There is an accusing glance that reveals what one is almost afraid to understand, a contrite, imploring glance that hardly encourages curiosity to peer into the involuntary telegraphy. As for reserve's content, all of this may in turn be quite comic, as when ridiculous things, frivolities, vanities, puerilities, expressions of petty envy, small medical obsessions, etc., reveal themselves in this way in involuntary anxiety.

The demonic is the sudden. The sudden is a new expression of reserve from another side. The demonic is defined as reserve when its content is reflected upon; reflection in terms of time defines it as the sudden. Reserve was the effect of the self-relation of denial in the individuality. Reserve shuts itself off ever more from communication. But communication is in turn the expression of continuity, and the negation of continuity is the sudden. One would think that reserve had an exceptional continuity; yet the very opposite is the case, although when compared with the vapid, soft-hearted dissipation of oneself that is constantly merging with the impression, it does have some appearance of continuity. Reserve's continuity can best be compared with the dizziness a spinning top can be imagined having when constantly revolving on its own tip. Where the reserve does not drive the individuality into total insanity, which is a sorrowful *perpetuum mobile* of sameness, the individuality will still keep up a certain continuity with the rest of human life. To this continuity, the pseudo-continuity of the reserve will make itself known precisely as the sudden. In one instant it is there, in the next it is gone, and no sooner is it gone than it is there again, whole and complete. It cannot be incorporated or worked into any continuity, but whatever expresses itself in this way is precisely the sudden.

If the demonic were something somatic, it would never be the sudden. When the fever or insanity, etc., keeps recurring, one does eventually come upon a law, and this law nullifies the sudden to a certain degree. But the sudden knows no law. It does not belong among natural phenomena; it is a psychic phenomenon, is unfreedom's utterance.

The sudden is, like the demonic, anxiety about the good. The good signifies continuity, since salvation's first expression is continuity. Thus, while the life of an individuality goes on in some degree of continuity with the rest of life, reserve maintains itself in the person as a continuity's abracadabra that communicates only with itself and therefore is always as the sudden.

Regarding reserve's content, the sudden may signify the terrible, but the effect of the sudden on the observer can also be comical. In this respect, every individuality has a little of this sudden, just as every individuality has something of a fixed idea.

I shall not pursue this further but, just to uphold my category I will recall to mind the fact that the sudden is always founded in anxiety about the good, because there is something that freedom will not permeate. Among the formations that lie in anxiety about evil, it will be weakness that corresponds to the sudden.

If one wants to clarify in some other way how the demonic is the sudden, then the question of how the demonic can best be presented may be considered in a purely aesthetical way. In a presentation of Mephistopheles, it is perfectly all right to give him some lines if, instead of being grasped in his character, he is to be used as an effective force in the dramatic action. But then Mephistopheles will not be really represented himself but dissolved into an evil, witty, intriguing mind. This however is a dispersion, whereas a folk legend has already seen it rightly. It tells that the devil sat for 3,000 years speculating on how to destroy man. He found out at last how. The emphasis here is on the 3,000 years, and the idea this elicits is precisely that of the demoniac's brooding reserve. If one wants not to disperse Mephistopheles in the way suggested, another form of representation may be chosen. Here it will appear that Mephistopheles is essentially mime.* Words of the most appalling kind sounding from the abyss of evil would be unable to produce an effect like that of the suddenness of the leap that lies in the scope of mime. Even if the words were terrible, even though it were a Shakespeare, a Byron, or a Shelley who broke the silence,[20] the word always retains its redeeming power, because all despair and all the horror of evil expressed in one word are not as awful as silence. Mimic can express the sudden yet without the miming itself therefore being the sudden. The ballet master Bournonville[21] deserves great credit in this respect for his representation of Mephistopheles. The horror that seizes one upon seeing Mephistopheles leap in through the window and remain stationary in the posture of the leap! This start, given by the leap, reminiscent of the bird of prey and the leap of the wild beast, doubly terrifying because it usually explodes from a quite stationary position, has an infinite effect. For this reason

---

*The author of *Either/Or* has pointed out that Don Giovanni is essentially musical. In just the same sense Mephistopheles is essentially mimical. The art of mime has gone the way of music. It is supposed that everything could become mimic and everything become music. We have a ballet called *Faust*. Had its composer really understood what it means to conceive Mephistopheles mimically, it would never have occurred to him to make a ballet of [Goethe's] *Faust*.

Mephistopheles must walk about as little as possible, for walking is itself a kind of transition to the leap, containing a hinted possibility of the leap. Mephistopheles's first appearance in the ballet *Faust* is therefore not a *coup de théatre* [cheap effect] but a very profound thought. The words and the speaking, no matter how short when regarded *in abstracto*, have always a certain continuity simply through being heard in time. But the sudden is a complete abstraction from continuity, from the past and from the future. So it is with Mephistopheles. We have yet to see him, and then there he stands, large as life, all of a piece, and the swiftness cannot be described more graphically than by saying that he stands there in a leap. If the leap goes over into a walk the effect is weakened. Represented in this way, Mephistopheles's entrance has the effect of the demonic that comes more suddenly than a thief in the night,* for the thief's approach is thought of as being stealthy. But Mephistopheles reveals his essence as well, which as the demonic is precisely the sudden. The demonic is thus the sudden in the forward movement, and this too is how it arises in the human being, this is how the human being itself is insofar as it is demonic, whether the demonic has possessed him wholly or there is only an infinitesimally small part of it in him. The demonic is always thus, and it is thus that unfreedom becomes anxious, and thus that its anxiety moves. Hence the tendency of the demonic toward mime, not in the sense of the beautiful but in the sense of the sudden, the abrupt, something that life often gives occasion to observe.

The demonic is the contentless, the tedious.

Having, in connection with the sudden, called attention to the aesthetic problem of how to represent the demonic, I shall now,

* [1 Thessalonians 5:2]

in order to throw light on what has been said, take up the same question once more. As soon as you put words into the demoniac's mouth and want to have him portrayed, the artist whose task it is to solve a problem of this kind will be clear about the categories. He knows that the demonic is essentially mimical: the sudden, however, is beyond his reach since it interferes with the lines. So he won't cheat, as if to blurt out the words, etc., would produce something like the true effect. So he correctly chooses the very opposite, the boring. The continuity answering to the sudden is what might be called extinction. Boredom, extinction, is a continuity in nothingness. The number in that legend can now be understood in a rather different way. The 3,000 years are not stressed to highlight the sudden; instead, the enormous span of time evokes the notion of the dreadful emptiness and vacuity of evil. Freedom is calm in continuity. Its opposite is the sudden, but also the calm that comes to mind when we see someone who looks as though long since dead and buried. An artist who grasps this will also see that, in discovering how to represent the demonic, he has found at the same time a way to express the comic. The comic effect can be produced in exactly the same way; for when all ethical attributes of evil are excluded, and only metaphysical attributes of emptiness are used, the result is the trivial, which easily lends itself to educing a comic effect.*

---

*The reason why [the Danish actor] little Winsløv's impersonation of Klister in [Heiberg's vaudeville] *The Inseparables* was so profound was that he had correctly understood the comical as the boring. The fact that a love affair, which when it is true has the nature of continuity, is exactly the opposite, namely, an infinite emptiness (not because Klister is an evil man, faithless, etc., since on the contrary he is sincerely in love, but because in his love affair he is a supernumerary volunteer, just as he is in the customhouse) has great comic effect when the accent is

The contentless, the boring, signify again the reserved. The reserved was a term that in connection with the sudden reflected on the essence. In now bringing in the contentless and the boring as an additional term, this reflects upon the essence and the reserved on the form corresponding to the essence. This completes the whole conceptual definition, since the form of contentlessness is precisely reserve. One must always bear in mind that, in my terminology, one cannot be reserved in God or in the good, since this kind of reservation signifies the greatest expansion. The more definitely conscience is developed in a person, then the more expanded he is, even though he otherwise closes himself off from the whole world.

If I were now to call to mind the terminologies of the most recent philosophy, I might say that the demonic is the negative and is nothing, just as the elf maid, who is hollow from behind.[22] However I prefer not to do this, because this terminology has become so obliging and pliable, in and through the company it keeps, that it can mean anything you please. The negative, if I were to use that word, would signify the form of nothing, just as the contentless corresponds to reserve. But the negative suffers the flaw of being more outwardly oriented, defining the relation to something else which is negated, while, as a term, the reserved defines the state itself.

If one wants to take the negative in that way, I have no objection to its use as a designation of the demonic, provided that the negative can otherwise put out of its head all the vagaries that the

---

placed on the boring. Klister's position itself in the customhouse could only be comic in an unfair way, because, good heavens, how could Klister help it that there is no promotion? But in relation to his love, there he is indeed his own master.

most recent philosophy has put into it. The negative has become by degrees a vaudeville figure, and that word always makes me smile, just as a person smiles when in real life or, for example, in the songs of Bellman,[23] he comes across one of those amusing characters who was first a trumpeter, later a minor customhouse officer, then an innkeeper, and then again a mailman. Irony has contrived in this way to be explained as the negative. First to hit on this explanation was Hegel, who oddly enough was himself no great judge of irony. That it was Socrates who first introduced irony into the world and gave the child a name, that his irony was precisely the reserve which began with his shutting himself off from others, shutting himself in with himself, so as to be expanded in the divine, and who also began by shutting his door and making fools of those outside in order to talk in secret,* this no one troubles themselves with. In the event of some or other accidental phenomenon someone brings up the word, and so it is irony. Then come the copycats who, in spite of their overview of world history, which unfortunately lacks all contemplation, know as much about the concepts as that noble youth knew about raisins, who, when asked in the test for his grocer's license where raisins come from, replied: We get ours from the professor on Tvergaden [Cross Street].

We return now to the definition of the demonic as anxiety about the good. If, on the one hand, unfreedom could close itself off completely and hypostatize itself but did not, on the other hand, constantly will to do so[†] (in this lies the contradiction that

---

* [Matthew 6:6]

† This must be constantly upheld despite the illusion of the demonic, and that of language usage, which in describing this state uses expressions that lead one almost to forget that unfreedom is a phenomenon of

unfreedom wills something when in fact it has lost its will), the demonic would not be anxious about the good. Therefore anxiety manifests itself most clearly in the moment of contact. Whether the demonic in the single individuality signifies the terrible, or whether the demonic is present only like a spot on the sun, or like the little white dot in the corn on one's foot, the totality of the demonic and the partly demonic have the same property, and the tiniest little part of the demonic is anxiety about the good in just the same sense as that which is totally enveloped by it. The bondage of sin is of course also unfreedom, but as explained above, its direction is another and its anxiety is about evil. Unless one insists on this, nothing can be explained. Unfreedom, the demonic, is therefore a state. That is how psychology considers it. Ethics on the other hand sees how, out of this state, the new sin constantly emerges, for only the good is the unity of state and movement.

Freedom may be lost, however, in different ways, with a corresponding difference in the demonic. This difference I shall now consider under the following headings: freedom lost somatopsychically, freedom lost spiritually [*pneumatisk*]. The reader must be already familiar from the foregoing with the fact that I take the concept of the demonic in a wide sense, though not, be it noted, more widely than the concept itself reaches. There is lit-

---

freedom and so cannot be explained by means of naturalistic categories. Even when unfreedom says, in the strongest possible terms, that it does not will itself, it is untrue and there is always a will in it that is stronger than the wish. This state can be extremely deceptive, for one can drive a person to despair by holding back and keeping the category pure in the face of his sophisms. One should not be afraid of this, but neither should youthful thought experimenters try themselves in these spheres.

tle point in making the demonic into a spook one first shudders
at but afterward ignores just because many centuries have gone
since it was found in the world. This assumption is a great stupidity; for it has perhaps never been as widespread as in our times,
only that nowadays it manifests itself particularly in the intellectual spheres.

i. Freedom lost somatopsychically

It is not my intention here to flaunt a high-flown philosophical
discussion on the relation between soul and body, in what sense
the soul itself produces its body (whether understood in the
Greek or the German way), or in what sense the soul itself by an
act of corporization, to recall an expression of Schelling's, posits
its body.[24] None of that is needed here; for my own purposes I
can express myself as best I can by saying that the body is the
soul's organ, and thus in turn that of spirit. Once this ministering relationship ceases, once the body revolts, and once freedom
conspires with the body against itself, unfreedom is present as
the demonic. Should anyone not yet have a clear grasp of the difference between what I have expounded in this section and what
was developed in the former, I state it here again. Once freedom
itself goes over to the side of the rebels, the anxiety of revolution
will indeed be present, but as anxiety about the good, not anxiety
about the evil.

It will easily be seen what multiplicity of innumerable nuances
the demonic includes in this sphere, some of which are so imper-
ceptible that they appear only to microscopic observation, and
some so dialectical that one must employ one's category with
great flexibility in order to see that the nuances belong under it.

A hypersensibility and a hyperirritability, neurasthenia, hysteria, hypochondria, etc., all of these are or could be nuances of it. This makes it so difficult to talk about these things *in abstracto*, since the talk itself becomes algebraic. But more than this I cannot do here.

The furthest extreme in this sphere is, and what is commonly called, bestial perdition. In this state, the demonic manifests itself by way of saying, as that demoniac in the New Testament did with regard to salvation: τί ἐμοὶ καὶ σοὶ [What have I to do with you]? Therefore it shuns every contact, whether this actually threatens by wanting to help it to freedom or even just comes in contact quite by accident. That too is enough, for anxiety is extraordinarily swift. It is therefore quite common to hear a line from a demoniac of this kind that contains all the horror of this state: Leave me alone in my wretchedness; or to hear one such say in referring to some particular moment of time in his past life: I could presumably have been saved then—the most dreadful reply imaginable. Neither punishment nor thunderous tirades will make him anxious but, on the contrary, every word that places itself in relation to the freedom that has been scuttled in unfreedom. There is also another way in which anxiety expresses itself in this phenomenon: Among such demoniacs one finds a solidarity in which they cling to one another so inseparably and anxiously that no friendship has an inwardness to compare with it. The French physician Duchatelet[25] provides examples of it in his work. And this sociability of anxiety will manifest itself everywhere in this sphere. The sociability contains by itself an assurance that the demonic is present, for to any degree in which the analogous state that expresses the bondage of sin is to be found, the sociability will not be manifest, because then the anxiety is about the evil.

I do not wish to pursue this further. Here the main thing for
me is simply to have my schema in order.

ii. Freedom lost spiritually [*pneumatisk*]

(a) *General remarks*. This form of the demonic is very widespread
and we meet here the most diverse phenomena. The demonic
is naturally not a question of the variety of the intellectual content but of the relation of freedom to the given content,[*] and to
the possible content regarding intellectuality, seeing that the
demonic can express itself as a laziness that postpones thinking,
as curiosity that never becomes more than that, as dishonest self-
deception, as effeminate weakness that constantly turns to others, or as superior negligence, as mindless busyness, etc.

Looked at intellectually, the content of freedom is truth, and
truth makes man free.[†] But that is exactly why truth works for
freedom in a way in which it constantly produces truth. I am
not, of course, thinking here of the brilliant thought of the most
recent philosophy, which maintains that thought's necessity is
also its freedom, and which therefore, when speaking of the freedom of thought, speaks only of the immanent movement of eternal thought. Such brilliance can serve only to confuse and pervert
communication between people. What I am speaking about, on

---

[*] In the New Testament there is the expression σοφία δαιμόνιώδης
[demonic wisdom] (James 3: 15). As it is described there, the category
does not become clear. However, if one takes note of the passage in
2:19, καὶ τὰ δαιμόνια πιστεύουσι καὶ φρίσσουσι [Even the demons believe
and shudder], one sees in precisely the demonic knowledge the relation
of unfreedom to the given knowledge.

[†] [John 8:32]

the contrary, is very plain and simple, namely, that truth for the particular individual is truth only insofar as the individual itself produces it in action. If truth is for the individual in any other way, or is prevented from being thus by the individual itself, we have a phenomenon of the demonic. Truth has always had many loud-voiced advocates, but the question is whether a person will in the deepest sense acknowledge the truth, will allow it to permeate his whole being, will accept all its consequences, and not, in an emergency, have a loophole for himself and a Judas kiss for the consequence.*

There has been enough talk recently about truth; it is high time now to vindicate certitude and inwardness, not in the abstract sense in which Fichte uses the word,[26] but in an altogether concrete way.

Certitude and inwardness, which can only be reached by and exist in action, decide whether or not the individual is demonic. One only keeps hold of the category and everything gives way, and it becomes clear that, for example, arbitrariness, unbelief, mockery of religion, etc., do not, as is commonly believed, lack content but lack certitude, in exactly the same sense as superstition, servility, and sanctimoniousness. The negative phenomena lack certitude precisely because they are in anxiety about the content.

I have no desire to speak in big words about the age as a whole, but anyone who has observed the present generation could hardly deny that its incongruousness, and the reason for its anxiety and unrest, is this, namely, that in one direction truth increases in scope, in quantity, partly also in abstract clarity, while in the opposite direction certitude is in constant decline. What extraordinary

* [Matthew 26:47–50; Luke 22:47–48]

metaphysical and logical efforts have been put into producing a new, an exhaustive, and an absolutely correct and summative proof of the immortality of the soul; and strangely enough, while this happens, certitude declines. The thought of immortality possesses a power, a pith in its consequences, a responsibility in its acceptance, which may perhaps transform the whole of life in a way that brings fear. And so one saves and soothes one's soul by straining one's mind to produce a new proof. What is such a proof but a "good work" in a purely Catholic sense? Every such individuality (to stay with the example) who knows how to produce evidence of the soul's immortality, but is not himself convinced, will always be anxious about every phenomenon whose effect on him is to force him to a further understanding of what it means to say that a person is immortal. It will disturb him. It will make an unpleasant impression on him when a perfectly simple person talks quite simply of immortality.

In the opposite direction there may be a lack of inwardness. An adherent of the most rigid orthodoxy may be demonic. He knows it all. He bows his head before the holy.* For him the truth is the aggregate of ceremonies. He talks of meeting before the throne of God† and knows how many times one is to bow. He knows everything, but like someone who can prove a mathematical proposition using the letters ABC, though not when they are DEF. So he becomes anxious whenever he hears something that is not the same to the letter. And yet, how much he resembles a modern speculator who has made out a new proof for the immortality of the soul and then, in peril of his life, was unable to pro-

* [Genesis 24:26]
† [Hebrews 4:16; "throne of grace"]

duce the proof because he did not have his notebooks with him. And what is it that both of them lack? It is certitude.

Superstition and unbelief are both forms of unfreedom. In superstition, objectivity is conceded a power—like that of Medusa's head[27]—to petrify subjectivity and unfreedom will not have the spell broken. The highest, seemingly freest, expression of unbelief is mockery. But the very thing that mockery lacks is certitude, and that is why it mocks. Yet how many a mocker's existence, if only we could look into it, would bring to mind the anxiety in which the demonic calls out: τὶ ἐμοί καὶ σοὶ [What have I to do with you]? It is therefore a matter of curiosity that perhaps few are as vain and touchy about the moment's applause as the mocker.

With what zealous industry, with what sacrifice of time, diligence, and writing materials the speculators in our time have worked at producing a complete proof of God's existence [Tilværelse]. Yet as much as the excellence of the proof increases, certitude seems correspondingly to decline. The thought of God's existence has, when posited as such for the individual's freedom, an omnipresence that for the prudish has, though they may have no thought of doing anything evil, something embarrassing about it. And it truly requires inwardness to live in a beautiful and intimate companionship with this conception, a much greater feat than that of being a model husband. How unpleasantly affected such an individuality may be on hearing this quite simpleminded and plain talk of there being a God; demonstrating God's existence is something with which one occupies oneself only occasionally, learnedly and metaphysically. But the thought of God will obtrude on every occasion. What is it that such an individuality lacks? Inwardness.

Inwardness may also be lacking in the opposite direction. The so-called holy are often the objects of the world's ridicule. They themselves explain this by saying that the world is evil. But that is not entirely true. If such a "holy" one is in an unfree relation to his holiness, that is, if he lacks inwardness, then he is, from a purely aesthetic point of view, simply comical. The world is in a way justified in laughing at him. If a bowlegged man wants to act as a dancing master but is unable to execute a single step, then he is comical. Similarly in the religious sphere. One may hear such a holy person as it were counting the beats to himself, just like someone who cannot dance but nevertheless knows enough to beat time though never lucky enough to get in step. Thus the "holy" one knows that the religious is absolutely commensurable, that it is not something belonging only to certain occasions and moments but something one can always have with one. But when he is on the point of making it commensurable, he is not free, and one notices that he is softly beating time to himself and that, in spite of everything, he puts a step wrong and makes a mess of his heavenward glance and folded hands, etc. That is why such an individuality is anxious to such a degree about everyone who is not trained in this way that, to give himself strength, he has to seize upon these grand observations about the world hating the pious.*

Certitude and inwardness, then, are indeed subjectivity, but not in an entirely abstract sense. It is altogether the misfortune of the newest knowledge that everything has become so terribly grand. Abstract subjectivity is just as uncertain and lacks inwardness to the same degree as abstract objectivity. This cannot be seen when one speaks about it *in abstracto*, and it will be cor-

* [Cf. John 17:14]

rect to say that abstract subjectivity lacks content. When spoken about *in concreto* it is clearly evident, for what the individuality that wants to make itself into an abstraction lacks is exactly inwardness, just like the individuality that makes itself into a mere master of ceremonies.

(b) *Schema for the exclusion or absence of inwardness.* The absence of inwardness is always attributed in reflection, and every form will therefore be a double form. Since people are accustomed to talking altogether abstractly about spirit's properties, perhaps they tend less to see this. Immediacy is usually posited in opposition to the reflection (inwardness), and then to the synthesis (or substantiality, subjectivity, identity, in whatever this identity is then said to consist: reason, idea, spirit). But in the sphere of actuality this is not how it is. There, immediacy is also the immediacy of inwardness. The absence of inwardness lies for this reason first of all in the reflection.

Every form of the absence of inwardness is therefore either activity-passivity or passivity-activity, and whether the one or the other, it rests in the self-reflection. The form itself runs through a considerable series of nuances according to the degree to which inwardness becomes more concrete. There is an old saying that understanding and to understand are two things, and so they are. Inwardness is an understanding, but *in concreto* it is a matter of how to understand this understanding. To understand a speech is one thing, understanding what is being pointed out to you is something else; to understand what you yourself are saying is one thing, understanding yourself in the saying is another. The more concrete the content of consciousness, the more concrete becomes the understanding, and as soon as it is absent to consciousness we have a case of unfreedom that wants to shut itself off from freedom. Thus, if we take a more concrete religious consciousness, which for that reason contains at the same time a historical factor, the understanding must stand in relation to this factor. We have an example here of the two analogous forms of the demonic in this respect. When a man of rigid orthodoxy applies all his diligence and learning to proving that every word in the New Testament derives from the respective apostle, inwardness will disappear little by little, and he comes in the end to understand something quite other than what he wanted to understand. When a freethinker[28] applies all his acumen to proving that the New Testament was not written until the second century, it is precisely inwardness he is afraid of, and for that reason he has to have the New Testament put in the same class with other books.* The most concrete content that consciousness can have

---

* In the religious spheres the demonic may even, moreover, bear an illusory resemblance to spiritual trial. What it is can never be decided *in abstracto*. Thus a pious and believing Christian may become anxious about going to Communion. This is a spiritual trial, which means that whether it is in fact that will appear in his relation to anxiety. A demonic nature, on the other hand, may have come so far, his religious consciousness become so concrete, that the inwardness about which he is anxious, and which in his anxiety he seeks to escape, is the purely personal understanding of the sacramental understanding. He is willing to go along with the latter only up to a certain point; then he breaks off and wants to relate to it only as one who knows, to be in one or another way something more than the empirical, historically defined, finite individuality that he is. One who is in the religious spiritual trial therefore wants to continue on to what it is that the spiritual trial holds him off from; while the demonic person, according to his stronger will (the will of unfreedom), wants to get away from it, while a weaker will in him wants to continue on. One must insist on this, otherwise the demonic comes to be conceived so abstractly as never to have occurred, as if the will of unfreedom were constituted as such, and the will of freedom were not always present, however weak, in the self-contradiction. Any-

is consciousness of itself, of the individual itself, not pure self-consciousness, but the self-consciousness that is so concrete that no author, not even one with the richest vocabulary, has ever been able to describe a single such self-consciousness, although every single human being is such a one. This self-consciousness is not contemplation, since anyone believing this finds that he has not understood himself on seeing that he is at the same time coming into being [i Vorden] and so cannot be something concluded for contemplation. This self-consciousness is therefore action, and this action in turn inwardness, and whenever inwardness does not correspond to this consciousness, there is a form of the demonic just as soon as the absence of inwardness expresses itself as anxiety about its acquisition.

If the absence of inwardness were brought about mechanically, all consideration of it would then be wasted effort. But neither is this the case, for in every appearance of the absence of inwardness there is an activity, even though this begins through a passivity. The phenomena that begin with activity are more conspicuous and one therefore grasps them more easily, forgetting then that in this activity a passivity again appears and never taking into account this contrasting phenomenon when talking about the demonic.

I shall now go through a few examples to indicate the correctness of the schema.

---

one wanting material on the religious spiritual trial will find it in abundance in [Johann Joseph von] Görres's *Mysticism*. I must frankly admit, however, that I have never had the courage to read the work properly from cover to cover; there is such an anxiety in it. But this much I can see, that Görres [1776–1848] does not always distinguish between the demonic and the spiritual trial. The work should therefore be used with care.

Unbelief–Superstition. These correspond to each other in every way; they both lack inwardness, but unbelief is passive through an activity, and superstition is active through a passivity. The one is, in a sense, the more masculine formation, the other the more feminine; the content of both is self-reflection. Essentially they are entirely identical. Unbelief and superstition are both anxiety about faith, but unbelief begins in the activity of unfreedom and superstition in the passivity of unfreedom. Usually it is only the passivity of superstition that is observed, and therefore it appears as less distinctive or more excusable, depending upon whether aesthetic-ethical or ethical categories are applied. There is a weakness in superstition that is engaging, but there must always be enough activity in it to keep its passivity going. Superstition is unbelieving about itself, unbelief is superstitious about itself. The content of both is self-reflection. The laziness, cowardice, and pusillanimity of superstition find it better to remain in self-reflection than to give it up. The defiance, pride, and arrogance of unbelief find it more daring to remain in self-reflection than to give it up. The most refined form of such self-reflection is always the one that becomes interesting to itself by wishing itself out of this state while remaining self-contentedly within it.

Hypocrisy–Offense. These correspond to each other. Hypocrisy begins through an activity, offense through a passivity. Generally, offense is judged more mildly, but if the individual remains in it there must be just enough activity for it to sustain the suffering of offense and not want to give it up. There is a receptivity in offense (for a tree or a stone is not offended) that is also taken into account in the nullifying of the offense. The passivity of offense finds it more pleasurable, on the other hand, just to sit and continue letting the consequence of the offense mount up as it were at compound interest. Hypocrisy is therefore offense at itself and offense hypocrisy toward itself. Both lack inwardness and dare not come to themselves. The reason why hypocrisy ends by being hypocritical toward itself is that the hypocrite is offended at himself or is an offense to himself. The reason why all offense, unless removed, ends in hypocrisy toward others is that the offended person, through the deep-seated activity by which he remains in offense, has turned that receptivity into something else and must therefore now be hypocritical toward others. It has also been the case in life that an offended individuality finally used this offense as a fig leaf* to cover what might otherwise have required hypocritical attire.

Pride–Cowardice. Pride begins through an activity, cowardice through a passivity; in all other respects they are identical, because in cowardice there is just enough activity to maintain anxiety about the good. Pride is a deep-seated cowardice, for it is cowardly enough not to be willing to understand what pride truly is. Once this understanding is forced upon it, it is cowardly, disintegrates with a bang and bursts like a bubble. Cowardice is a deep-seated pride, for it is cowardly enough not to be willing to understand even the misunderstood pride's demands, and shows its pride precisely by hanging back in this way, as well as by bringing into account the fact of never having suffered a defeat, and is therefore proud of pride's negative expression, namely, that it has never suffered any loss. The case has also occurred in life of a very proud individuality being cowardly to the point of never risking anything, cowardly enough to be as insignificant as possible, precisely in order to save its own pride. If an active-proud and a

* [Cf. Genesis 3:7]

passive-proud individuality are brought together, precisely in the moment when the former fell there would be an opportunity to be convinced of how proud the cowardly one really was.*

(c) *What are certitude and inwardness?* Giving a definition of inwardness is no doubt hard. But for the time being I shall say that it is earnestness. This is a word that everyone understands, but strangely enough, few words have been less frequently subject to discussion. When Macbeth murdered the king, he exclaimed:

> *Von jetzt giebt es nicht Ernstes mehr im Leben:*
> *Alles ist Tand, gestorben Ruhm und Gnade!*
> *Der Lebenswein ist ausgcschenkt.*

[From this instant / There's nothing serious in mortality; / All is but toys; renown and grace is dead: / The wine of life is drawn.][29]

---

*In his treatise *De affectionibus* [On the Passions] Descartes [Renatus Cartesius (1596–1650), the French rationalist philosopher] calls attention to the fact that to every passion there corresponds another passion, and that only with wonder is this not the case. The detailed exposition is rather weak, but his making an exception of wonder has roused interest, because as is well known, according to Plato's and Aristotle's concept, precisely this constitutes the passion of philosophy and the passion with which all philosophizing began. Moreover, corresponding to wonder [*admiratio*; Kierkegaard here implies a slightly different sense of *admiratio*] we have envy, and no doubt recent philosophy would also speak of doubt. In just this lies the fundamental mistake of recent philosophy, that it wants to begin with the negative instead of with the positive, which is always the first, in quite the same sense as *affirmatio* is placed first in the declaration *omnis affirmatio est negatio* [every affirmation is a negation]. The question of whether the positive or the negative comes first is exceedingly important, and really the only modern philosopher who has declared himself for the positive is [Johann Friedrich] Herbart [1776–1841].

Certainly Macbeth was a murderer. The words in his mouth were therefore a dreadful and shocking truth. Yet every individual who has lost inwardness can also say: "*der Lebenswein ist ausgeschenkt*," and also for that matter, "*jetzt giebt es nichts Ernstes mehr im Leben, Alles ist Tand*," for inwardness is just that fountain that gushes up to eternal life,* and what issues from this fountain is precisely earnestness. When the preacher says in Ecclesiastes that "all is vanity,"† earnestness is exactly what he has in mind. When, on the other hand, after earnestness is lost, it is said that all is vanity, then this is but an active-passive expression for the same (the defiance of melancholy), or a passive-active expression (the defiance of frivolity and witticism), and then there is either occasion to weep or to laugh,‡ but earnestness is lost.

So far as I know, there is no single definition of earnestness. It would please me if there were none, not because I love the fluency and confluence of modern thinking that has abolished the definition, but because with regard to existential concepts it always betrays greater discretion to abstain from definitions, seeing that one is hardly inclined to grasp in the form of definition the essential in what must be understood in another way, what one has oneself understood in another way, has loved in an entirely different way, and which easily becomes in the form of a definition something alien, something else. Anyone who truly loves can hardly find joy and satisfaction, not to mention further growth, in being preoccupied with a definition of what love properly is. Whoever lives in daily, and yet solemn, communion with the thought

* [John 4:14]
† [Ecclesiastes 1:2]
‡ [Ecclesiastes 3:4]

that there is a God, could hardly wish himself to pervert this, or see it perverted, by patching together his own definition of what God is. So too with earnestness, which is so earnest a matter that even a definition of it is a frivolity. This is not something I say as though my thinking were obscure, or because I am afraid that one or another superwise speculator—who is as bullheaded in developing concepts as the mathematician is in the proof, and who says about everything what a certain mathematician said: So what does this prove?—should be suspicious of me, as though I didn't really know what I was talking about. To my mind, what I say here proves much better than any conceptual development that I know in all earnestness what is being discussed.

Though inclined not to give a definition of earnestness, or to talk about it in the jest of abstraction, I shall nevertheless present some remarks by way of orientation. In Rosenkranz's *Psychologie*[*30] there is a definition of *Gemyt* [disposition, or temperament]. He says on page 322 that disposition is the unity of feeling and self-consciousness. Before that he superbly explains *"daß das Gefühl zum Selbstbewußtsein sich aufschließe, und umgekehrt, daß*

---

*It gives me pleasure to assume that my reader has read as much as I. This assumption is very economical for the reader as well as for the writer. So I assume that my reader is familiar with the book to which I have referred. If not, then I urge him to familiarize himself with it, for it is really competent, and if the author, who otherwise distinguishes himself by his common sense and his humane interest in human life, had been able to renounce his superstitious enthusiasm for an empty schema, he might have avoided being occasionally ridiculous. What he says in the presentation sections is for the most part very good. The only thing not always understandable is the grandiose schema and how the altogether concrete presentation can answer to it. (As an example, I refer to pp. 209–11. *Das Selbst—und das Selbst:* 1. *Der Tod;* 2. *Der Gegensatz von Herrschaft und Knechtschaft.*)

der Inhalt des Selbstbewußtseins von dem Subjekt als der seinige *gefühlt wird. Erst diese Einheit kann man Gemüth nennen. Denn fehlt die Klarheit der Erkenntniß, das Wissen vom Gefühl, so existirt nur der Drang des Naturgeistes, der Turgor der Unmittelbarkeit. Fehlt aber das Gefühl, so existirt nur ein abstrakter Begriff, der nicht die letzte Innigkeit des geistigen Daseins erreicht hat, der nicht mit dem Selbst des Geistes Eines geworden ist* [that the feeling unfolds itself to self-consciousness, and vice versa, that the content of the self-consciousness is felt by the subject as his own. It is only this unity that can be called disposition. If the clarity of cognition is lacking, knowledge of the feeling, there exists only the urge of the spirit of nature, the turgidity of immediacy. On the other hand, if feeling is lacking, all that remains is the abstract concept that has not reached the last inwardness of the spiritual existence, that has not become one with the self of the spirit]" (cf. pp. 320, 321). If one now follows his definition of "feeling" again in the reverse direction, as the spirit's *unmittelbare Einheit seiner Seelenhaftigkeit und seines Bewußtseins* [immediate unity of its sentience and its consciousness] (p. 242), and recalls that in the definition of *Seelenhaftigkeit* [sentience] account has been taken of the unity with the immediate character of nature, then by taking all of this together one has a conception of a concrete personality.

Earnestness and disposition correspond to each other in such a way that earnestness is a higher and the deepest expression of what it is to be a disposition. The disposition is an immediate property, while earnestness is on the contrary the disposition's acquired primitivity, its preserved primitivity in the responsibility of freedom, its affirmed primitivity in the enjoyment of blessedness. The primitivity of disposition in its historical development indicates precisely the eternal in earnestness, for which reason earnestness can never become habit. Rosenkranz deals with habit only in the "Phenomenology," not in the "Pneumatology." However, habit belongs there too, and habit arises as soon as the eternal drops out of the repetition. When the primitivity in earnestness is acquired and kept, there is succession and repetition, but as soon as primitivity is lacking in the repetition, there is habit. The earnest man is earnest precisely through the primitivity with which he returns in repetition. It is said that a living and inward feeling preserves this primitivity, but the inwardness of the feeling is a fire that may cool once earnestness no longer tends it, and on the other hand, the inwardness of feeling is uncertain in its mood, that is, at one time it is more inward than at another. I take an example so as to make everything as concrete as possible. Every Sunday a clergyman must recite the prescribed common prayer, and every Sunday he baptizes several children. Let him now be enthusiastic, etc. The fire goes out, he wants to stir and move people, etc., but more at one time and less at another. Earnestness alone is capable of returning to the same thing regularly every Sunday with the same primitivity.*

But this same thing to which earnestness is to return with the same earnestness can only be earnestness itself; otherwise it becomes pedantry. Earnestness, in this sense, means the personality itself, and only an earnest personality is an actual personality, and only an earnest personality can do something in earnest,

---

* It was in this sense that Constantin Constantius (in *Repetition*) said, "Repetition is the earnestnessness of existence" [*Tilværelse*], p. 6 [Repetition *and* Philosophical Crumbs, trans. Piety, p. 4] and that the earnestness of life is not to be like a royal riding-master, even if such a man every time he mounted his horse, did so with all possible earnestness.

for to do anything in earnest requires, first and foremost, knowledge of what the object of earnestness is.

In life one talks not infrequently of earnestness. Someone becomes earnest about the national debt, another about the categories, and a third about a performance at the theater, etc. Irony discovers that this happens and has enough to occupy itself with here, since anyone who becomes earnest at the wrong place is *eo ipso* comical, even though an equally comically travestied contemporary age and its opinion may be exceedingly earnest about it. There is, therefore, no measuring rod more accurate for determining what, in its deepest core, an individuality is capable of than what one learns through the individual's own garrulity or by tricking this secret out of him: What is it that made him earnest in life? For although one may very well be born with disposition, one is not born with earnestness. The phrase "What has made him earnest in life?" must of course be understood in a pregnant sense, as that from which the individuality in the deepest sense dates his earnestness. For having become truly earnest about that which is the object of earnestness, one may very well treat various things earnestly if one will, but the question is whether one first became earnest about the object of earnestness. This object is something every human being has, because it is *himself,* and anyone who has not become earnest about this but about something else, something great and noisy, that person, despite all his earnestness, is a joker, and even if he can deceive irony for a time, he will *deo volente* [God willing] still become comical, for irony is jealous of earnestness. He who, on the other hand, has become earnest at the right place will prove his soundness of mind precisely by being able to treat everything else just as sentimentally as jokingly, even if the spines of those serious-looking fools run

cold when they see him joke about what made them so fright-
fully earnest. But when it comes to earnestness, he will know not
to tolerate any joke, for if he forgets this he may share the fate
of Albert Magnus when he arrogantly boasted of his speculation
before the deity:* he suddenly became stupid. Or that of Bellero-
phon, who sat calmly on his Pegasus in the service of the idea, but
fell off when he wanted to misuse Pegasus by riding the horse to
a rendezvous with a mortal woman.[31]

Inwardness, certitude, is earnestness. This looks a little paltry. If I had at least said: It is subjectivity, the pure subjectivity, the *übergreifende* [encompassing] subjectivity; then I would
have said something, something that would no doubt have made

---

*Cf. Marbach, *Geschichte der Philosophie*, pt. 2, p. 302, note: *Albertus
repente ex asino factus philosophus et ex philosopho asinus* [Albert was
suddenly transformed from an ass into a philosopher and from a philosopher into an ass]. Cf. Tennemann, VIII, pt. 2, p. 485, note. There is an
even more distinctive account of another scholastic, Simon Tornacen-
sis, who thought that God must be obliged to him for having proved the
Trinity; for if he wanted, then *profecto si malignando et adversando vel-
lem, fortioribus argumentis scirem illam infirmare et deprimendo impro-
bare* [if I wanted out of spite and enmity to do so, I could weaken it (the
proof) with stronger arguments, and disprove it by reducing them]. As
reward for his pains, the good man was turned into a fool who had to
spend two years learning the alphabet. See Tennemann, *Geschichte der
Philosophie*, VIII, B, p. 314, note. Be this as it may, and whether he
actually said this or even uttered what has been ascribed to him—the
famous blasphemy of the Middle Ages about the three great deceivers
[Moses, Christ, and Muhammed]—certainly what he lacked was not
strenuous earnestness in dialectics and speculation but, rather, an
understanding of himself. There are no doubt enough analogies to this
story to be found, and in our day speculation has assumed such authority that it has well nigh attempted to make God feel uncertain of himself, like a monarch who anxiously waits to learn whether the general
assembly will make him an absolute or a constitutional monarch.

many earnest. But earnestness is something I can also express in another way. As soon as inwardness is lacking, the spirit is finitized. Inwardness is therefore eternity or the constituent of the eternal in the human being.

To study the demonic properly one need only observe how the eternal is construed in the individuality and one will be immediately informed. In this respect, the modern age offers a broad field for observation. The eternal is discussed often enough in our time; it is accepted and rejected, and (considering the way in which this is done) the first shows lack of inwardness just as much as the second. But anyone who has not understood the eternal correctly, understood it altogether concretely, lacks inwardness and earnestness.[*]

I do not wish to go to any great length here but will indicate some points.

(a) One denies the eternal in man. That same moment the *Lebenswein* is *ausgeschenkt* [the wine of life is drawn] and every such individuality is demonic. If the eternal is posited, the present becomes something other than what one wants. This prompts fear and one is then in anxiety about the good. A person can go on denying the eternal as long as he will, but in doing so he will not do away with the eternal altogether. And even if one will admit the eternal to some degree, and in a certain sense, one fears that other sense and that higher degree. Yet however much one denies it, one will not be entirely rid of it. The eternal is feared far too much in our time, even when it is recognized in the abstract and in what, for the eternal, are flattering terms. While the various

---

[*] It was no doubt in this sense that Constantin Constantius said of the eternal that it is the true repetition [Repetition *and* Philosophical Crumbs, trans. Piety, p. 75].

governments live nowadays in fear of restless troublemakers, only all too many individualities live in fear of a restless troublemaker that is nevertheless true calm—for eternity. Then one preaches the moment, and just as the road to hell is paved with good intentions, so is eternity best destroyed by sheer moments. But why are people in so terrible a hurry? If there is no eternity, the moment is just as long as if there were. But anxiety about the eternal makes the moment into an abstraction.—What is more, this denial of the eternal can express itself directly or indirectly in a great variety of ways, as mockery, as a prosaic intoxication with common sense, as busyness, as enthusiasm for the temporal, etc.

(b) The eternal is construed altogether abstractly. Like the blue mountains, the eternal is the boundary of the temporal, but he who lives energetically in temporality never reaches the boundary. The single individual who spies out beyond is a frontier guard who stands outside time.

(c) Eternity is bent into time for the imagination. Construed in this way, eternity produces an enchanting effect. It does not know whether it is dream or actuality; the eternal peeps wistfully, dreamily, roguishly into the moment, as the beams from the moon glimmer in an illuminated forest, or a hall. Thought of the eternal becomes a fanciful busying, and the mood is always the same: Am I dreaming, or is it eternity that dreams about me?

Or it is construed purely for the imagination, unmixed with this coquettish duplicity. This construal has found definite expression in the maxim: Art is an anticipation of eternal life. For poetry and art are reconciliation only for the imagination, and may well have the *Sinnigkeit* [thoughtfulness] of intuition, but by no means the *Innigkeit* [inwardness] of earnestness. The eternal is elaborated in the gold-leaf tinsel of the imagination and then yearned for. Apocalyptically, one beholds eternity, plays at being

Dante, while Dante, no matter how much he conceded to visions of imagination, did not suspend the effect of ethical judgment.

(d) Eternity is construed metaphysically. One keeps on saying *Ich - Ich* [I—I][32] until one becomes that most ridiculous thing of all: the pure I, the eternal self-consciousness. One keeps on talking at such length about immortality that, in the end, one becomes not immortal, but immortality. Despite all this, the discovery is suddenly made that immortality has been brought into the system, and people are then intent on finding a place for it in a supplement. In consideration of this ludicrousness, what Poul Møller said is true, that immortality must be present everywhere.[33] But if that is so, then the temporal itself becomes something quite other than what one wants. Or eternity is metaphysically construed in such a way that the temporal becomes comically preserved in it. From a purely aesthetic-metaphysical point of view, the temporal is comical because it is a contradiction, and the comical always rests in that category. If eternity is conceived purely metaphysically, and one wants for some reason or other to include the temporal in it, then indeed it becomes quite comical that an eternal spirit retains the memory of several times having been in financial difficulties, etc. Yet all of this effort expended on upholding eternity is wasted and a false alarm, for no human being becomes immortal, or convinced of his immortality, in a purely metaphysical way. But if he becomes convinced of it in quite another way, the comic will not force itself upon him. Even though Christianity teaches that a person must render an account for every idle word that he has spoken,* and we understand this simply as a general recollection, of which unmistakable symptoms can occasionally appear already in this life, and even if no sharper

---

* [Matthew 12:36]

light can be thrown on the teaching of Christianity than by the contrast offered by the Greek construal, that the immortals first drank of Lethe in order to forget,[34] it still by no means follows that recollection must become directly or indirectly comical—directly by recollecting ridiculous things, or indirectly by transforming ridiculous occasions into essential decisions. Precisely because the accounting and the judgment are essential, this essentiality will have the effect of a Lethe on whatever is inessential, while it is also certain that many things will prove essential that one never believed would be so. In life's drolleries, its accidental circumstances, its odd nooks and crannies, the soul has not been essentially present. Hence all this vanishes except for that soul who was in this essentially, but for him it will hardly acquire comical significance. If one has reflected thoroughly upon the comical, studying it in practice, keeping one's category constantly clear, it will readily be understood that the comical belongs of all things to the temporal, for that is where the contradiction is found. One cannot stop it, metaphysically and aesthetically, and prevent it from finally swallowing whole the temporal, which will happen to someone developed enough to use the comic but not mature enough to distinguish *inter et inter* [between one and the other]. In eternity, on the other hand, all contradiction is canceled, the temporal is permeated by and preserved in the eternal, but in it there is no trace of the comical.

But eternity is not what people think earnestly about; they are anxious about it, and anxiety can hit on a hundred evasions. Yet this is precisely the demonic.

V

—

Anxiety as Saving through Faith

In one of Grimm's folktales there is a story of a young man who went out in search of adventure in order to learn what it is to be anxious.[1] We will let the adventurer follow his own path without worrying whether he came across the horror on his way. I will however say this, that it is an adventure that every human being has to live through, learning to be anxious so as not to be ruined either by never having been in anxiety or by sinking into it. Whoever has learned to be anxious in the right way has learned the ultimate.

As a beast or an angel, a human being could not be made anxious. Through being a synthesis the human being can be made anxious, and the more profoundly, the greater the human being. Not, however, in the usual sense in which anxiety is about something external, about something outside a person, but in the sense that it is the person himself who produces the anxiety. Only in this sense can the words be understood when it is said of Christ that he was grieved unto death,* as well as the words Christ spoke

---

* [Matthew 26:37; Mark 14:33]

to Judas: Do quickly what you are going to do.* Not even the terrifying verse that made Luther himself anxious when preaching on
it: "My God, my God, why have you forsaken me?"† not even these
words express suffering as strongly. For what these latter signify
is a condition Christ finds himself in, the former a relation to a
condition that *is* not.

Anxiety is freedom's possibility; this anxiety alone is, through
faith, absolutely formative, since it consumes all finite ends, discovers all their deceptions. And no Grand Inquisitor has such
frightful torments in readiness as has anxiety, and no secret agent
knows as cunningly how to attack the suspect in his weakest
moment, or to make so seductive the trap in which he will be
snared; and no discerning judge understands how to examine,
yes, exanimate [*exanimere*: dishearten],² the accused as does anxiety, which never lets him go, not in diversion, not in noise, not at
work, not by day, not by night.

Anyone formed by anxiety is shaped by possibility, and only
the person shaped by possibility is cultivated according to his
infinitude. Possibility is therefore the most difficult of all categories. It is true that we often hear the opposite, that possibility is so
light, while actuality is so heavy. But from whom do we hear such
words? From a few wretches who do not know what possibility is,
and who, when they were shown by actuality that they were good
for nothing and always would be, had mendaciously spruced up
a possibility that was then ever so fine, so enchanting, and this
possibility was at bottom no more than a little youthful frivolity of
which one should rather be ashamed. The possibility said to be so

* [John 13:27]
† [Mark 15:34]

light is usually thought of as the possibility of happiness, good fortune, etc. But this, absolutely, is not possibility; it is a lying invention that human depravity has tricked up in order to have some
reason to complain at life, and at Governance,[3] and an occasion
to be self-important. No, in possibility all things are equally possible and anyone truly brought up by possibility has grasped the
terrifying just as well as the smiling. So when a person like this
graduates from the school of possibility, and knows better than a
child knows its ABCs that absolutely nothing can be demanded
of life, and that horror, perdition, and annihilation live next door
to every human being, and when he has thoroughly learned that
every anxiety for which he feels alarm can come upon him the
very next instant, then he will give actuality another explanation.
He will praise actuality, and even when it lies heavily upon him
he will remember that it is still far, far lighter than possibility had
been. Only in this way can possibility shape a person, because
finiteness and the finite situations, in which every individual is
assigned its place, whether they be small or commonplace or
world historical, are only finitely formative: one can always talk
them over, always get something a little else out of them, always
bargain, always come a little out of their way, always keep oneself
a little on the outside, always prevent oneself from learning something absolutely from them. But if the individual is to do that, the
individual must again have possibility in itself, and shape by itself
that from which it is to learn, even if in the next instant this latter
by no means acknowledges that it is shaped by the individual but
takes from the individual its power absolutely.

But for an individual to be formed thus absolutely and
infinitely by possibility, that individual must be honest toward
possibility and have faith. By faith, I understand here what Hegel

somewhere, characteristically and very rightly, calls the inner certainty that anticipates infinity. When the discoveries of possibility are honestly administered, possibility will discover all finitudes but idealize them in the shape of infinity, in anxiety overwhelm the individual, until the individual again overcomes them in the anticipation of faith.

What I say here may to many seem obscure and foolish talk, since they pride themselves on never having been in anxiety. To this I would reply that one should certainly not be in anxiety about persons, about finitudes; only someone who passes through the anxiety of the possible is cultivated to have no anxiety, not because this person can escape the terrible things of life, but because these always become weak by comparison with those of possibility. If, on the other hand, the speaker maintains that the great thing about him is that he has never been in anxiety, I will gladly provide him with my explanation: that it comes from his being very spiritless.

By cheating possibility, which molds the individual, an individual never arrives at faith; the faith will be a finitude's sagacity, just as that individual's school was one of finitude. But people cheat possibility in every way. Otherwise just by sticking their neck out of the window everyone would have seen enough for possibility to begin its maneuvers. There is an engraving by Chodowiecki representing the surrender of Calais as viewed by the four temperaments,[4] and the artist's task was to have the various impressions reflected in the facial expressions of the temperaments. No doubt the most commonplace life has experiences enough, but the question is that of possibility in the individuality that is honest with itself. It is told of one Indian hermit, who for two years lived on dew, that he came one time to the city, tasted wine and took to drink. As with similar stories, this one can be understood in many ways. It can be made comic, it can be made tragic. But the individuality formed by possibility needs but one such story. That individual, in that very instant, is absolutely identified with that unfortunate. He knows no finite subterfuge whereby to escape. In him the anxiety of possibility now has its prey, until, saved, it must hand him over to faith. Nowhere else can he find rest, for every other resting place is only chatter, although in people's eyes it is sagacity.

You see then how possibility for this reason is absolutely formative. No one ever became so unhappy in actuality as not to retain a little residue, and common sense quite correctly says that if one is clever, then one knows how to make the best of it. Yet the person who followed possibility's curriculum in misfortune lost everything in a way that no one in actuality ever lost it. But then, unless he cheated the possibility that wanted to teach him, and did not talk onto his side the anxiety that wanted to save him, he would also receive everything back* as no one else in actuality ever did, even if they received everything tenfold, for the disciple of possibility received infinity, and the soul of the other expired in the finite.

No one sank so deep in actuality as to be unable to sink deeper, or so deep that another or many others have not sunk deeper. But that person who sank in possibility, that person's gaze became giddy, his eye became blurred so that he could not catch hold of the yardstick that Tom, Dick, and Harry reach out as a straw for the drowning man to grasp, and his ear was closed so that he did not hear what the market price for human beings was

*[Job 42:10]

in his day, did not hear that he was just as good as most. He sank down absolutely, but then he rose up again from the abyss, lighter than all that is oppressive and dreadful in life. Except that I won't deny that the one who is formed by possibility is exposed, not as those formed by finitude to coming into bad company, excesses of various kinds, but to downfall, and that is suicide. If, on the point of being formed, he misunderstands the anxiety, so that it leads him not *to* faith but away from it, then he is lost. On the other hand, someone who is already formed remains with anxiety; he does not allow himself to be deceived by its countless falsifications; he accurately remembers the past. The attacks of anxiety, even though terrifying, will then not be such that he flees from them. Anxiety becomes for him a ministering spirit that leads him, against its will, where he will.* Then, when it announces itself, when it disingenuously makes it look as though it has invented an altogether new instrument of torture, far more terrible than anything before, he does not draw back, and still less does he try to ward it off with noise and confusion, but bids it welcome, greets it solemnly, and like Socrates who raised the poisoned cup, he takes it in with him and says, as a patient would say to the surgeon, when the painful operation is about to begin: Now I am ready. Then anxiety enters into his soul and searches out everything, and frightens the finite and petty out of him, and it then leads him where he will.

When one or another extraordinary event occurs in life, when a world-historical hero gathers heroes about him and performs heroic deeds, when a crisis occurs and everything takes on meaning, then people want to have a part in it, for this is formative.

---

* [John 21:18]

Quite possibly. But there is a far handier way to become formed, and formed far more thoroughly. Take the disciple of possibility, place him in the middle of the Jutland heath, where nothing happens, or where the biggest event is a grouse noisily taking wing, and he experiences everything more perfectly, more accurately, more thoroughly than someone who was applauded on the stage of world history, that is, if he was not yet formed by possibility.

So when the individual, through anxiety, is formed to faith, anxiety will then eradicate what it itself produces. Anxiety discovers fate, but when the individual would entrust itself to fate, anxiety switches around and takes fate away; for fate, like anxiety, and anxiety, like possibility, is a witch's letter.[5] If the individuality is not transformed by itself with regard to fate, it will always retain a dialectical remnant that no finitude can do away with, any more than a person will lose faith in the lottery who does not lose it through himself but because he keeps on losing. Even regarding the most trivial things, anxiety is promptly on hand as soon as the individuality wants to sneak off from something, take a chance on something. In itself, this something is a triviality, and from outside, from the finite, the individual can learn nothing about it. But anxiety makes short work of it, instantly playing the trump card of infinity, of the category, and the individuality cannot take the trick. An individuality like that cannot fear fate with its vicissitudes and defeats in an outward way, because the anxiety within him has already fashioned fate and has taken away from him absolutely all that any fate could take away. In the dialogue *Cratylus*,[6] Socrates says that it is terrible to be deceived by oneself, because one always has the deceiver with one. Similarly, one may say that it is fortunate to have with one a deceiver like that who piously deceives and always weans the child before finitude begins to make a mess of it. So far as, in our time, an individuality is not shaped by possibility in this way, this time of ours nevertheless has an excellent attribute for each one in whom there is a deeper nature and who desires to learn the good. The more peaceful and quiet an age, the more accurately everything follows its regular course so that the good has its reward, so much the easier it is for an individuality to deceive itself about its striving not having a goal, however beautiful it may be, that is nevertheless finite. In these times of ours, on the other hand, one need be no more than sixteen years old to see that whoever is now about to play a part on the stage of life's theater is just like the man who traveled from Jericho and fell among robbers.*

Anyone not wanting to sink in the wretchedness of the finite is obliged in the most profound sense to struggle with the infinite. Such a preliminary orientation is analogous to the formation by possibility, and such an orientation cannot take place other than through possibility. So when shrewdness has completed its countless calculations, when the gamble succeeds, then anxiety comes along even before the game in actuality has been lost or won, and anxiety makes the sign of the cross against the devil and shrewdness can do nothing, and its cleverest combinations vanish like a pleasantry opposite the case formed by anxiety with the omnipotence of possibility. Even in the most trifling things, once the individuality wants to make a clever turn that is only clever, wants to sneak away from something, and there is every likelihood that it will succeed, since actuality is not as sharp an examiner as anxiety, then anxiety is there. If the trifle is dismissed because it is only a trifle, then anxiety makes this trifle as prominent as that

---

* [Luke 10:30]

speck of a place Marengo became in the history of Europe because the great battle of Marengo was fought there. If an individuality is not weaned away from shrewdness by itself, then it will never occur properly, because finitude always explains piecemeal, never totally, and the person whose shrewdness always fails (and even this is unthinkable in actuality) may look for the reason in the shrewdness and then strive to become still shrewder. With faith's help, anxiety educates the individuality to rest in providence. So too in respect of guilt, which is the second thing anxiety discovers. Those who learn to know their guilt only from the finite are lost in the finite, and finitely the question of whether a person is guilty cannot be determined except in an external, juridical, most imperfect sense. The person who learns to know guilt only by analogy to judgments of the police court and the supreme court, never really understand that he is guilty, for if a person is guilty, the guilt is infinite. If such an individuality, who is formed only by finitude, fails to receive a verdict from the police or from public opinion pronouncing guilt, that individuality becomes something that is the most ridiculous and pitiful of all, a model of virtue that is little better than most people but not quite as good as the parson. What help should such a man need in life, when he can retire to a cabinet collection of examples almost before he dies? From finitude one can learn much, but not how to be anxious, except in a very mediocre and corrupting sense. Anyone who has truly learned how to be anxious, on the other hand, will tread as if in a dance when the anxieties of finitude strike up, and when finitude's apprentices lose wit and courage. Life often deceives in this way. The hypochondriac is anxious about everything unimportant but begins to breathe more easily when something important comes along. And why? Because the important actuality is not as terrible after all as the possibility he himself had fashioned, and which he used his strength to fashion, instead now of being able to use all his strength against actuality. The hypochondriac is, however, but an imperfect autodidact compared with the person who is cultivated by possibility, because hypochondria depends partly on the somatic and is consequently accidental.* The true autodidact is in exactly the same degree a theodidact,† as another author has said,‡ or to use an expression less redolent of the intellectual, he is αὔτουργος τὶς τῆς φιλοσοφίας [one who cultivates philosophy on his own] and in the same degree θεουργος [one who tends the things of God]. Therefore the person who, in respect of guilt, is educated by anxiety will rest only in the Atonement.

Here this deliberation ends where it began. Once psychology has finished with anxiety, it is to be handed over to dogmatics.

---

* So it is with a higher meaning that Hamann employs the word "hypochondria" when he says: *"Diese Angst in der Welt ist aber der einzige Beweis unserer Heterogeneität. Denn fehlte uns nichts, so würden wir es nicht besser machen als die Heiden und Transcendental-Philosophen, die von Gott nichts wissen, und in die liebe Natur sich wie die Narren vergaffen, kein Heimweh würde uns anwandeln. Diese impertinente Unruhe, diese heilige Hypochondrie ist vielleicht das Feuer, womit wir Opferthiere gesalzen und vor der Fäulniß des laufenden seculi bewahrt werden müßen* [However, this anxiety in the world is the only proof of our heterogeneity. If we lacked nothing, we should do no better than the pagans and the transcendental philosophers, who know nothing of God and like fools fall in love with lovely nature, and no homesickness would come over us. This impertinent disquiet, this holy hypochondria, is perhaps the fire with which we season sacrificial animals in order to preserve us from the putrefaction of the current *seculum* (century)]," I (vol. 6, p. 194).

† Thessalonians 4:9; "θεοδίδακτοί"]

‡ See *Either/Or*.

Notes

Translator's Introduction

1. Friedrich Wilhelm Joseph von Schelling, *System des transzendentalen Idealismus* (Tübingen, 1800); *System of Transcendental Idealism*, trans. Peter Heath (Charlottesville: University of Virginia Press, 1997).

2. Georg Wilhelm Friedrich Hegel, *Phenomenology of Spirit*, trans. A. V. Miller (Oxford: Clarendon Press, 1977), §80, p. 51.

3. Georg Wilhelm Friedrich Hegel, *Faith and Knowledge*, trans. W. Cerf and H. S. Harris (Albany: State University of New York Press, 1977), p. 58.

4. *Kierkegaard's Journals and Notebooks* (hereinafter *KJN*), ed. Niels Jørgen Cappelørn et al. (Princeton: Princeton University Press, 2008), vol. 2, JJ:511.

5. Søren Kierkegaard, *Fear and Trembling*, trans. Alastair Hannay (London: Penguin Books, 1985), p. 83 (*Great Ideas* edition, 2005, p. 63).

6. *Søren Kierkegaard* Repetition *and* Philosophical Crumbs, trans. M. G. Piety, Intro. Edward F. Mooney (Oxford: Oxford University Press, 2009), p. 173.

7. *Kierkegaard's Papers and Journals: A Selection*, trans. Alastair Hannay (London: Penguin Books, 1996), pp. 185–86.

8. *The Sickness unto Death*, a sequel to *The Concept of Anxiety* at a later time when Kierkegaard had become an open defender of his radical Christianity, suggests that the stress we place on finite achievement, fortune, fame, and respectability, a stress so great that we feel ruined when misfortune or disability intervenes, signals a "despair over ourselves." This is not despair at not having become Caesar, it is the despair manifested in wanting to become Caesar in the first place, that of replacing an infinite with a finite wish (*The Sickness unto Death*, trans. Alastair Hannay [London: Penguin Books, 1989], p. 49 [*Great Ideas* edition, 2008, p. 17]).

9. *Søren Kierkegaards Skrifter* (hereinafter *SKS*), ed. Niels Jørgen Cappelørn et al. (Copenhagen: Gads Forlag, 2003), vol. 20 NB:123; *Kierkegaard's Papers and Journals: A Selection*, trans. Hannay, p. 254.

10. *Søren Kierkegaard* Repetition *and* Philosophical Crumbs, trans. Piety, p. 172.

Translator's Note

1. For details of the preparation of the text and its publication I have drawn on the account given in *SKS*, vol. K(ommentarbind)4, pp. 317–39.

2. Walter Lowrie, "How Kierkegaard Got into English," in *A Short Life of Kierkegaard* (Princeton: Princeton University Press, 2013 [1942]), p. 279.

3. Ellsworth Faris, *American Journal of Sociology* 50 (1945): 401.

4. Abraham Myerson, MD, *The American Journal of Psychiatry* 1945 (101): 839.

5. *KJN* 1, JJ:227 (1844).

6. *KJN* 5, NB 10:29 (1849) (translation altered); *Kierkegaard's Papers and Journals: A Selection*, p. 365.

Preface

1. An alternative preface originally intended for this work appeared as "Preface No. 7" in *Prefaces*, published in the same month as *The Concept of Anxiety* and *Philosophical Crumbs*. Kierkegaard may have dropped it because of its unduly polemical remarks on local writers (see the commentary volume K4 in *SKS*, p. 552). That Preface says that, instead of trying to understand all men, he has chosen what people may regard as a "narrow and foolish aim," namely to understand himself, a task in which progress is likely to be "slower" (*SKS* 4, pp. 501–2).

2. A reference to a proposed annual publication designed by its editor and publisher J. L. Heiberg to appear at the beginning of the year as a "New Year's present." The foremost cultural personality in Copenhagen at the time, Heiberg was writer, critic, editor, and also effective popularizer of Hegel, whose lectures he had attended. Famous for his vaudevilles modeled on the French theater, Heiberg was married to Denmark's most celebrated actress Johanne Louise Pätges, whom Kierkegaard much admired and was the subject of his "The Crisis and a Crisis in an Actress's Life" from 1847. In 1846 Heiberg became director of the Royal Theater in Copenhagen. Largely due to Heiberg's somewhat disdainful reviews of his publications, Kierkegaard rarely passed up an opportunity to belittle this gifted man, whose satirical gifts were equal to his own. Heiberg's comedy "A Soul after Death" (1841) is thought to have prompted the title of Kierkegaard's *The Sickness unto Death* (1849).

3. Latin, "let it be printed," the censor's permission (still required of religious works in Catholicism) before publication. In *Erasmus Montanus or Erasmus Berg*, a comedy by the Norwegian-Danish writer Ludwig Holberg (1684–1754). The expression is understood by one character to refer to a person.

Introduction

1. A reference to Georg Wilhelm Friedrich Hegel's *Wissenschaft der Logik* (*Science of Logic*), where "Actuality [Wirklichkeit]" is in fact the topic of the second book's third section, its second chapter in particular.

2. A reference to Hegelians who take faith to be in part an immediate relation to God that is to be replaced by speculative knowledge (see Translator's Introduction).

3. Hegel's logic begins with pure being or "indeterminate immediacy" (*Science of Logic*, ch.1, §1).

4. The reference is to local Danish writers such as A. P. Adler, who published popularized versions of Hegel (1770–1831) and particularly of his "speculative" logic.

5. An ideal of Absolute or Transcendental Idealism most characteristically presented in Friedrich Wilhelm Joseph von Schelling's *System des transzendentalen Idealismus* (Tübingen 1800); *System of Transcendental Idealism*, trans. Peter Heath. On Schelling (1775–1854) see Translator's Introduction.

6. Immanuel Kant (1724–1804) held that experience obeys its own object-giving laws and that therefore anything that lies beyond experience ("things in themselves") cannot be known. Just as the Scottish philosopher David Hume (1711–1776) motivated Kant's arrival at laws guaranteeing the objective reference of experience, so Kant provoked Schelling and Hegel into finding a way to bring things-in-themselves within cognitive range.

7. The phrase "Method and Manifestation" may be due to A. P. Adler's "propaedeutic" writing on Hegel.

8. Usually associated with the Hegelian dialectic in which the negation of one notion produces its opposite and the resulting opposition or "contradiction" between them is then overcome by virtue of reason's coming upon a more encompassing notion that contains elements of both, as, for example, in the case of necessity and freedom, where true freedom will not be abstract and arbitrary but situated and dependent. As in much of Hegel and Schelling, the terminology is largely due to Kant.

9. The proper doctrine of the Word, as announced in the first words of the Gospel of St. John: "In the beginning was the Word, and the Word was with God, and the Word was God." The Greek for "word" is λόγος from which the term "logic" is derived.

10. Ethics in Protestant theology has traditionally to do with the Christian way of life and dogmatics with the content of Christian faith.

11. Hegel's notion of *Aufhebung* (Danish *ophævelse*), meaning "abrogate" or "abolish," but in Hegel with the special sense as in note 8 of preserving what is "annulled" or "nullified" in a higher, more encompassing notion. See Hegel's *Science of Logic*, vol. 1, part 2, ch. 3.

12. *Science of Logic*, vol. 7, bk. 7, §§ 1, II B.

13. Anne Louise Germaine de Staël-Holstein (1766–1817), the famous Mme de Staël, who wrote to this effect in *Über Deutschland* (On Germany).

14. That Hegelian philosophy, often referred to as the System, was on its way to completion, if not already complete in principle, is something Kierkegaard constantly ridicules.

15. "Mood" is one of many notions that Kierkegaard will have found in his reading of the German Hegelian Karl Rosenkranz, *Psychologie oder die Wissenschaft vom subjektiven Geist* [Psychology or the science of subjective spirit] (Königsberg, 1837).

16. *Nicomachean Ethics*, bk. 1, ch. 8.

17. Anaximander (c. 610–c. 546 BC), a pre-Socratic Greek philosopher now considered by many the forerunner of scientific thinking and noted for his idea that ultimate reality is *apeiron* (unlimited, infinite, indefinite). He introduces the unexplained notion of a vortex motion to account for the separation of heavier from lighter elements.

18. Friedrich Daniel Ernst Schleiermacher (1768–1834) was Romanticism's leading theologian and had many followers in Copenhagen, including Kierkegaard's philosophy teacher, F. C. S. Sibbern, before the overwhelming influence of Hegel made itself felt among younger thinkers.

19. Concupiscence (Latin, *concupisco*: strive after), originally any desire of the soul for the good, but in wider use a desire of the lower appetites.

20. In his *Metaphysics* Aristotle used this term for philosophy concerned with first causes and ultimate principles.

21. A reference to the German mathematician and rationalist philosopher Gottfried Wilhelm Leibniz (1646–1716), *Les principes de la Philosophie ou la Monadologie* (Monadology; c. 1713).

22. When Syracuse was taken by the Romans (212 BC), Archimedes, the most famous of ancient mathematicians and natural philosophers, was killed while concentrating on a mathematical problem.

Chapter I

1. Also known as covenant theology: a framework in Calvinism from the seventeenth century that interprets the Bible (from creation to consummation) under the concepts of works, grace, and redemption. Before the Fall there is covenant of nature (innocence) in which Adam goes proxy for humankind, but after that Fall this is no longer within that covenant and Christ then becomes a requirement of fulfillment.

2. The Smalcald Articles: Martin Luther's summary of Lutheran doctrine written in 1537 for an ecumenical council of the Church.

3. Quintus Septimus Florens Tertullian(us) (c. AD 160–230). Born in Carthage, North Africa, and son of a Roman centurion, Tertullian was one of the earliest Church Fathers and a fierce opponent of worldiness in the Church as also of speculation in religious matters.

4. St. Augustine (Augustinus Aurelius), the Church Father, born AD 354 in Numidia, educated at Carthage, and famous for his *Confessions* and *De Civitate Dei*. He died when bishop of Hippo, in 430, when the city was besieged by Vandals.

5. Abbreviation of *Apologia Augustinae Confessionis* (really *Apologia Confessionis Augustanae*) by the German reformer, and close colleague of Luther, Philipp Melanchthon (1497–1560).

6. *Formula Concordiae* (Formula of Concord; 1577) is the final authoritative statement of Lutheran faith (its creed), and was designed to heal a split in the early days of the Lutheran Church.

7. Uncompromising laws named after Dracon, the seventh-century BC Athenian legislator who established a written code of laws (said to be

written in blood rather than ink) in which death was the penalty for almost every transgression. His laws fell into disuse after Solon's legislation (594 BC).

8. Pelagianism: the Pelagian heresy, due to Pelagius (c. 354–425), possibly an inhabitant of Britain or Ireland, to the effect that human nature is unaffected by the belief in hereditary sin and that the mortal will is able to choose good or evil without divine aid. Socinianism: named after Fausto Sozzini (1539–1604), it denies Christ's full deity and hence the Trinity, hereditary sin, and the inability of self-conversion. Versions are found today in Unitarians and the Jehovah's Witnesses. Philanthropic singular: Johann Bernhard Basedow (1724–1790), educational reformer, founded the progressive Philanthropinum school in Dessau. Kierkegaard would perhaps know of him through Basedow's appointment in the previous midcentury to the progressive Sorø Academy in Denmark, funded by Ludwig Holberg (see Preface, note 3). Basedow had been a popular teacher in religion and literature.

9. In J. L. Heiberg's vaudeville *Recensten og Dyret* (The critic and the beast), a sixty-year-old law student, Trop, says that it is at least something that he can offer proof of having almost passed the Latin exam.

10. Boys at the Royal Charity School.

11. Ethical rigorism is usually associated with Kant and the familiar example he draws from his "categorical imperative," that it is wrong to lie in whatever circumstances. In Church history it goes back to ascetic movements, some of them regarded as heresies, such as the Montanism espoused by Tertullian himself (see note 3, above) in his later years.

12. The Danish refers to a clip used to close off a sausage, calling to mind the Danish expression *at koge suppe paa en pølsepind* (to cook sausage from a sausage pin). A stingy woman is said to have offered to make soup from such a clip for a wanderer, while the latter offers richer suggestions including the sausage, from which the sense of "spinning a long yarn" is derived.

13. Leonhard Usteri (1799–1833), a Swiss Protestant theologian and educator strongly influenced by Schleiermacher. The reference is to

Usteri's *Entwicklung des Paulinischen Lehrbegriffe in seinem Verhält-nisse zur biblischen Dogmatik des Neuen Testamentes. Ein exegetisch-dogmatischer Versuch* (Development of the Pauline concept of teaching in its relation to the New Testament's scriptural dogmatics), Zürich 1824, a work that Kierkegaard possessed.

14. Cambyses, second king of Persia, who reigned from 529–522 BC, in order to overcome the strong defense of the Egyptian city of Plurion in 525, placed before it examples of species of animals they considered holy, thus causing its defenders to stop using their catapult machines.

15. It is tempting but probably incorrect to translate "alle katholsk-fortjenstlige Phantasterier" as "all Catholic self-serving whimsies," inde-pendently of a reference to Adam's alleged superior merit.

16. The other in this case is not another person or self, but simply other.

17. In a draft for this passage Kierkegaard writes that, as far as he knows, scientists have concluded that animals are not anxious, only afraid of what they meet. The sense in which they are not anxious is captured in a familiar poem by the Scottish poet Robert Burns "To a Mouse": "Still thou art blest, compar'd wi me! / The present only toucheth thee: / But och! I backward cast my e'e, / On prospects drear! / An forward, tho' I canna see, / I guess an fear!" From what was said in the Translator's Introduction it is clear that the anxiety for things absent denied to the mouse is still not the topic of the present work.

18. The Danish expressions may be more natural than these English language near-equivalents.

19. The commentators in *SKS*, K4 (p. 416) suggest that Gabriel was the saint that Kierkegaard had in mind. It is true that Michael's "mission" (as protector of the Jews) was of a more military manner than the con-text suggests here.

20. *Die kluge Else* (Wise Else): a tale from the folklore collected by the Brothers Grimm.

21. Salomon Soldin, a bookseller in Copenhagen about whom such sto-ries were rife.

Chapter II

1. In Chapter IV, §2.

2. In §2 (B) of the present chapter.

3. In a journal entry referred to in the Translator's Note (note 5) regarding the pseudonym, Kiekegaard writes: "The sketch I dashed off of an observer in *The Concept of Anxiety* will probably upset some people. However, it does belong there and is a kind of watermark in the work . . . Simultaneously with the book's development of some themes, the corresponding individuality is drawn. Now Vigilius Hauf. draws several, but in the book I have dashed off a sketch of him in addition" (*KJN* 2, JJ:227).

4. Chapter IV, "Sin's Anxiety or Anxiety as the Outcome of Sin in the Single Individual."

5. Eighteenth-century rationalist philosophers (notably Descartes, Leibniz, and Spinoza) claimed that the acquisition of knowledge, including that of religious truths, was accessible to unaided though properly used reason.

6. Franz Xavier von Baader (1765–1841), German Roman Catholic philosopher, also a trained engineer who spent some years in England. Finding the philosophical atmosphere there not to his taste, he had turned to Schelling and wrote in an aphoristic style thoughts that he also owed to the mystic Jakob Boehme (1575–1624).

7. Pelagianism. See Chapter I, note 8.

8. In Ludwig Holberg's comedy *Erasmus Montanus or Rasmus Berg*, Hieronymus's daughter writes to Erasmus that her father refuses to give her away to him until he renounces his belief in the roundness of the earth.

9. Ganymede, perhaps less generally heard of than these other figures in Greek mythology, was a beautiful young Trojan hero abducted by Zeus to be a cup-bearer in Olympus.

10. For *Scham* (German, "shame").

11. Friedrich von Schlegel (1772–1829), a central figure in the German Romantic movement and responsible for converting the notion of irony as a mere figure of speech into an entire literary or quasi-philosophical perspective that names Socrates among its antecedents and has Kierkegaard among its main exponents. The reference is to Schlegel's "Geschichte des Zauberers Merlin" (History of the Magician Merlin).

12. Xenophon (b. c. 444 BC): Greek historian, mercenary, and philosopher. Allegedly a student of Socrates's, to whom it is also said he owed his life at the battle of Delium (424). His account of Socrates in *Memorabilia*, defending Socrates against corrupting the Athenian youth, is usually regarded as reliable.

13. One at variance with current scientific classifications. An example in Kierkegaard's time was an unusually large tadpole that was considered a hybrid between a frog and a salamander that developed into a fish.

14. In theology "pneumatics" (Greek *pneuma*—spirit, breath, wind) refers to doctrine or issues concerning the soul or spirit.

15. "Know yourself!" The inscription on the Temple of Apollo at Delphi in Greece.

Chapter III

1. Member of ancient Greek sect who practiced gazing at the navel as a means of inducing hypnotic reverie.

2. Danish *Kaffémølle*: lit. coffee grinder, a term used for a simple two-wheeled wagon typical of the countryside, while the chosen translation here refers to an old-fashioned two-wheeled chaise or else any old-fashioned and worn-out vehicle.

3. From *Frithiofs Saga*, a poem cycle by the Swedish writer Esaias Tegnér from 1825.

4. In Plato's *Phaido* Socrates tries to show that the soul is immortal through the notion of learning. Kierkegaard uses this notion as a con-

trast to his own (one could say Christian existentialist) notion that truth is in the making and thus in the future rather than in a retrievable past.

5. Socrates and Hamann (cf. the epigraph to *Anxiety* and Translator's Introduction).

6. The electrical basis of nerve impulses and stimulation of muscles was demonstrated with a frog in 1789 by the Italian scientist and physician Luigi Galvani (1737–98), to whom the verb "galvanize" in its everyday and technical or scientific uses is due.

7. Marengo in northern Italy where in 1800 the French forces under Napoleon defeated the Austrians prior to Napoleon's assuming the position of First Consul in Paris.

8. The location in 1805 of one of Napoleon's greatest victories, this time over combined Russian and Austrian forces.

9. A quotation from Plutarch (c. AD 46–c. 120). See *Plutarch's Lives*, vol. 2 (London: Dent/New York: E. P. Dutton, 1910), p. 559.

10. Charles Maurice de Talleyrand-Périgord (1754–1838), French diplomatist sometimes thought to be the most skilled in history but also suspected of treason to all the movements over which he had influence. He left the Catholic Church after being ordained.

11. Carpocrates was a second-century BC Alexandrian Gnostic who held that one could only be free from all sin by first trying everything including the sins.

12. Pamphilius of Caesarea, a fourth-century biblical scholar known for his generosity as well as his wealth and his death by torture.

13. The English poet Edward Young (1681–1765): "Where Nature's end of language is declined / and men talk only to conceal their mind" (*Night Thoughts*).

14. Hegel divides concepts into those that are immediately derivable from experience and those that are formed by a reflection that reaches their essence.

Chapter IV

1. Renderings in Greek, Latin, and French of the notion of "idle argument" or "lazy reasoning" attributed by the Roman orator Cicero (106–43 BC) to the Greek Stoic philosopher Chrysippus (c. 280–c. 207 BC) and recorded also in Leibniz's *Theodicy*, a work to which Kierkegaard frequently refers.

2. In the last scene of Act 2 of Mozart's opera *Don Giovanni*.

3. Sometimes called the "doodlebug" due to the doodling trails it leaves while looking for a place to make its trap.

4. Probably a reference to Schelling's *System des transcendentalen Idealismus* (see Introduction, note 5).

5. Shakespeare, *King Lear*, Act 4, scene 6, Gloucester to Lear: "O ruin'd piece of nature! This great world / Shall so wear out to nought." Kierkegaard translates as usual from the German translation by A. W. Schlegel and I. Tieck, *Shakespeare's dramatische Werke*, Berlin, 1839–41.

6. In ancient Greece Scythia was an indeterminate area north of the Black Sea inhabited by nomad peoples who were expert in cavalry exercises and archery.

7. "in terms of the idea": looked at from the standpoint of the concept.

8. Johann Gottlieb Fichte (1762–1814), "elder" in relation to his son the "younger" Immanuel Hermann Fichte (1797–1879) whom Kierkegaard also read. The comment here is due to a reference made by Kierkegaard's contemporary and in many ways rival, the Danish theologian, moral philosopher, and later Danish primate Hans Lassen Martensen (1808–84).

9. Johann Caspar Lavater (1741–1801), Swiss Protestant pastor and founder of physiognomics.

10. It seems that Augustine did not in fact recommend the death penalty, although this is thought to be true of Tertullian.

11. E.T.A. Hoffmann (1776–1822), an all-round German Romantic writer of horror and fantasy, composer, and jurist.

12. Brutus in Shakespeare's *Julius Caesar* (1623), and Henry V as Prince of Wales, in Shakespeare's *Henry IV*, parts 1 and 2 (1597–98).

13. Accepting the sacraments in communion.

14. The expression in Danish translates as "out with the language [*ud med Sproget!*]."

15. A Danish saying. Also "Every devil reigns in his time, but Our Lord reigns always."

16. From a Danish saying to the effect that fools have their hearts on their tongues and the wise their tongues in their hearts.

17. Titus Flavius Domitian(us) (51–96), a Roman Emperor with totalitarian tendencies; Oliver Cromwell (1599–1658), uncompromising Protestant Lord Protector of the Commonwealth of England; Fernando Alvarez de Toledo Alba (1508–82), despotic Spanish general represented in Goethe's *Egmont*; the head of the Jesuit Order was known as a Jesuit general.

18. A device formerly made of wickerwork that helps children to learn to walk while supported; similar in principle to a "walker."

19. In Shakespeare's *Hamlet*, Act I, scene 2: "And whatsoever shall hap to-night, / Give it an understanding, but no tongue." Here from Schlegel and Tieck's German translation.

20. The Romantic poets George Gordon (Lord) Byron (1788–1824) and Percy Bysshe Shelley (1792–1822).

21. August Bournonville (1805–79), world famous choreographer, solo dancer, and mimer at the Royal Danish Ballet.

22. In legend a fairy that looks full bodied *en face* but proves hollow as a "kneading trough" from behind.

23. Carl Michael Bellman (1740–95), Swedish poet and songwriter, composer, and performer.

24. Cf. F. W. J. Schelling, *Philosophische Untersuchungen über das Wesen der menschlichen Freiheit und die damit zusammenhängenden Gegenstände* (1809), translated by Jeff Love and Johannes Schmidt as *Philosophical Investigations into the Essence of Freedom* (Albany, NY: State University of New York Press, 2007).

25. Alexandre Jean Baptiste Benjamin Parent-Duchatelet, a French physician and hygienist mentioned in Rosenkranz's *Psychologie oder die Wissenschaft vom subjektiven Geist* (Königsberg, 1837).

26. A likely reference to J. G. Fichte's *Wissenschaftslehre*. Cf. *Grundlage der gesamten Wissenschaftslehre* (1794/95; 2nd ed., 1802). *Foundations of the Entire Science of Knowledge*, trans. Peter Heath. In *Fichte: Science of Knowledge (Wissenschaftslehre)*, ed. Peter Heath and John Lachs (New York: Appleton-Century-Crofts, 1970); 2nd ed. (Cambridge: Cambridge University Press, 1982).

27. Medusa, one of three fearsome maidens known as Gorgons, the others being Stheno and Euryale. Their heads were covered in serpents instead of hair, although in Medusa's case only after Athena had punished her in this way for using one of her temples to conceive Chrysaor and Pegasus. All who looked at her head were turned to stone.

28. Perhaps Bruno Bauer (1809–82) in his two volume *Kritikk der evangenlischen Geschichte der Synoptiker* (Critique of the Evangelical history of the Synoptics [the Gospels of Matthew, Mark, Luke, and John]; Leipzig 1841–42).

29. Kierkegaard quotes directly from Schlegel and Tieck's translation, which is in this case quite direct. The English version provided here is from an accredited edition of Shakespeare.

30. Karl Rosenkranz, *Psychologie oder die Wissenschaft vom subjektiven Geist* (Königsberg, 1837).

31. Albertus Magnus (1193–1220), German theologian and philosopher in Paris and Cologne who wrote extensively on Aristotle.

32. J. G. Fichte's theory that the conscious subject is the sole ground for the explanation of all experience and that consciousness of any object of experience is implicitly consciousness directed toward itself as origin.

33. A reference to an essay on the possibility of proving immortality by Poul Martin Møller, *Anxiety*'s dedicatee (see Translator's Introduction).

34. "Lethe" is a word which in Ancient Greek, like the Latin "oblivio," means "forgetfulness." It was the name given to the river of oblivion in the lower world from which the shades drank in order to lose their memory of the past.

Chapter V

1. Jakob L. K. Grimm and Wilhelm K. Grimm, *Kinder- und Hausmärchen* [Children's and Household Tales], vol. 1, no. 4.

2. This is where, in preparing the second edition, the typesetter mistook a near pun for a double occurrence of the same word. See Translator's Introduction.

3. Governance (Danish *Styrelse*): God's governance, a notion allied to that of Providence and sometimes translated "Guidance."

4. Daniel Nikolaus Chodowiecki (1726–1801), a Polish German painter and printmaker. The picture in question appears as an illustration in a work by Lavater (Physiognomische Fragmente, vol. 4). See Chapter IV, note 9.

5. Danish *Hexebrev*, a set of picture parts of animals and people that that can be "magically" combined in different ways.

6. In Plato's dialogue *Cratylus*, 428d.

Concordance

The figures on the right of the columns refer to lines on pages in Volume 4 of *Søren Kierkegaards Skrifter* (Copenhagen 1997) on which the Danish text of first lines of pages of this translation appear (e.g., 313,1 = page 313, line 1).

Preface		25	325,1	42	340,18	61	355,9	78	368,2
7	313,1	26	327,5	43	341,18	62	355,1	79	368,25
		27	328,15	44	342,14	63	356,27	80	369,23
Contents		28	329,6	45	343,5			81	370,13
1	315,1	29	330,5	46	343,36	Chapter II		82	371,2
		30	330,32	47	344,24	64	357,1	83	371,30
Introduction				48	345,18	65	357,18	84	372,21
13	317,1	Chapter I		49	346,3	66	358,16	85	373,14
14	317,21	31	332,1	50	347,6	67	359,6	86	374,2
15	318,22	32	332,20	51	347,28	68	359,34	87	374,8
16	319,14	33	333,19	52	348,22	69	360,25	88	375,21
17	320,4	34	334,4	53	349,15	70	361,17	89	376,17
18	320,15	35	334,27	54	350,7	71	362,20	90	377,6
19	321,28	36	335,23	55	350,28	72	363,3	91	377,33
20	322,13	37	336,18	56	351,18	73	364,1	92	378,22
21	323,14	38	337,4	57	352,8	74	364,5	93	379,16
22	324,1	39	338,9	58	353,1	75	365,21	94	380,8
23	324,33	40	339,1	59	353,20	76	366,15	95	381,2
24	326,18	41	339,20	60	354,15	77	367,5	96	381,27

97	382,10	117	398,34	137	415,18	159	433,2	181	449,15
98	383,16	118	399,24	138	416,11	160	433,29	182	450,9
		119	400,18	139	417,7	161	434,16	183	451,3
Chapter III		120	401,9	140	417,35	162	435,15	184	451,27
99	384,1	121	401,35	141	418,25	163	436,1	185	452,23
100	384,20	122	402,25	142	419,18	164	436,22	186	453,13
101	385,19	123	403,17	143	420,4	165	437,24		
102	386,25	124	404,7	144	420,27	166	438,17	Chapter V	
103	386,1	125	404,36	145	421,21	167	439,10	187	454,1
104	388,6	126	405,26	146	422,13	168	439,34	188	454,16
105	389,4	127	406,19	147	423,3	169	440,22	189	455,14
106	390,27	128	407,13	148	424,1	170	441,13	190	456,5
107	390,28	129	408,1	149	424,28	171	442,3	191	456,32
108	391,8	130	408,25	150	425,18	172	442,29	192	457,19
109	392,17	131	409,25	151	426,11	173	443,4	193	458,9
110	393,9	132	410,17	152	427,3	174	444,14	194	459,36
111	394,2	133	411,10	153	427,29	175	445,5	195	459,25
112	394,30			154	428,12	176	445,30	196	460,17
113	395,13	Chapter IV		155	429,14	177	446,9		
114	396,9	134	413,1	156	430,16	178	447,13		
115	397,19	135	413,14	157	431,11	179	448,4		
116	398,9	136	414,6	158	432,6	180	448,21		

About the Author

Søren Aabye Kierkegaard, was born on May 5, 1813, to an affluent family in Copenhagen, Denmark. He was educated at the School of Civic Virtue, before entering the University of Copenhagen. Showing no clearly focused academic interests in the seven years he spent there, but reading widely and recording his thoughts in journals, he gained a reputation for both academic brilliance and an extravagant social life. In 1841, after breaking off an engagement with his then fiancée, Regine Olsen, Kierkegaard fully devoted himself to writing. Over the next ten years, he would go on to produce numerous discourses and a dozen major philosophical works—including *Either/Or* (1843), *Repetition* (1843), *Fear and Trembling* (1843), *Philosophical Crumbs* (1844), *The Concept of Anxiety* (1844), *Stages on Life's Way* (1845), *Concluding Unscientific Postscript* (1846), and *The Sickness Unto Death* (1849)—many of which, like these, were written pseudonymously. During this period, however, Kierkegaard had not only begun to openly criticize the Danish State Church but he also provoked a sustained feud with the *Corsair*, a satirical Danish weekly. As a result, Kierkegaard became an object of public ridicule. While few mourned his death in the autumn of 1855, during the early twentieth century his body of work underwent a renaissance and became a major force in shaping modern Protestant theology and existentialism. Today, Kierkegaard is widely considered to be the father of both existentialism as well as modern psychology and has attracted increased attention from academics in a wide range of disciplines.

About the Translator

Alastair Hannay (b. 1932) is an emeritus professor of philosophy at the University of Oslo, has been a visiting professor at the University of California (Berkeley and San Diego) and the University of Stockholm, and was for many years editor of *Inquiry*. He is the author of *Mental Images: A Defence* (Allen & Unwin 1971; Routledge 2002), *Kierkegaard* (Routledge 1982, 1999), *Human Consciousness* (Routledge 1990), *Kierkegaard: A Biography* (Cambridge 2001), *Kierkegaard and Philosophy* (Routledge 2003), and *On the Public* (Routledge 2005). He has already translated several of Kierkegaard's works (for Penguin Classics and Cambridge University Press) and is engaged in the ongoing Princeton critical edition of Kierkegaard's *Papers and Journals*. A resident of Norway since 1961, he is a Fellow of the Royal Society of Edinburgh, of the Royal Norwegian Scientific Society of Science and Letters, and of the Norwegian Academy of Science and Letters.